# HOW TO PASS EXA

**In this Series**

How to Avoid a Heart Attack
How to Choose a Private School
How to Claim State Benefits
How to Enjoy Retirement
How to Get a Job Abroad
How to Get That Job
How to Help Your Child at School
How to Keep Business Accounts
How to Live & Work in America
How to Live & Work in Australia
How to Master Public Speaking
How to Prepare Your Child for School
How to Raise Business Finance
How to Run a Local Campaign
How to Start a Business from Home
How to Study Abroad
How to Succeed in Teaching
How to Survive at College
How to Teach Abroad
How to Use a Library
How to Write for Publication

*other titles in preparation*

**How To Books** General Editor Roland Seymour

# PASS EXAMS
## WITHOUT ANXIETY

## David Acres

**Northcote House**

© *Copyright 1987 by David Acres*

First published in 1987 by Northcote House Publishers Ltd,
Harper & Row House, Estover Road,
Plymouth PL6 7PZ, United Kingdom
Tel: Plymouth (0752) 705251. Telex: 45635

Reprinted 1988

**British Library Cataloguing in Publication Data**

Acres, David
  How to pass exams without anxiety—
  2nd ed.—(How to books)
  1. Study, Method of
  I. Title
  371.3′028′12      LB1049

  ISBN 0-7463-0334-3


*Printed and bound in Great Britain by
Biddles Ltd, Guildford and King's Lynn*

# Contents

# Acknowledgements

The ideas in this book owe much to the hundreds of students, teachers and parents who've contacted me to tell me how well the ideas work in practice. 'How to Pass Exams without Anxiety' is the result of those many helpful comments on 'Exams without Anxiety', successfully published in 1984. The ideas in the original remain largely unaltered but I've added to them a number of new ones. For example, Margaret Boulden has suggested a remedy for sleeplessness; Robert Lees has alerted me to how certain eye movements improve recall and spelling; and Roma Thomas, my Yoga teacher, has helped this particularly amateurish performer refine a number of the breathing and relaxation techniques in this book.

I'd also like to thank Roger Ferneyhough for the detailed work which has given this book its clear, easy-to-use layout and Roland Seymour, for his unflagging support and encouragement.

Finally I'd like to acknowledge the contributions to the original text of John Jenkinson, Susan Kyrke-Smith, Kate Acres, Dave Thorpe, Angela Harris, Paul Barrett and Wini Coles. Support and useful critical comments have been offered by Peter Aizlewood, Sandra Allitt, Stephanie Bromley, George and Vanessa Buckton, Mark Brockbank and my family Carol, Kate and John.

# 1
# How to Use this Book

A step-by-step guide
The importance of asking questions
Your questions about this book
My questions about this book

# How to use this book

**First step**

Read **The Importance of Asking Questions** before going any further. The ideas on *these two pages are the most important in this book.* It is important to read them if you wish to make the best use of this book. Look through the **Contents** and/or **Your Questions about this book** to give you an overall view of what the book contains and immediately after read **The Importance of Asking Questions** before reading any further.

**Second Step**

Find out more about what the book contains and if it meets your needs by looking quickly through the **Contents, Your Questions about this book** and the **Problem Checklists — Revision — Taking Exams** and — **Coping with Anxiety.** As you do so, ask yourself the question 'Which parts of the book could be useful to me?' Tick any headings or topics which seem relevant to you as you look through it. This book is designed to be *used.* If it is yours, write on it as much as it helps.

**Third Step**

Go through the particular Problem Checklist of most immediate concern to you. As you read through that Checklist again, more slowly, ask yourself 'Have I or may I have this problem?', ticking the box provided, if the answer is 'Yes'. Work your way through to the end of the Checklist, continuing to tick wherever the answer is 'Yes' to the question.

If your particular problem does not appear in the Checklist, check the **Contents** and **Index** and turn to the appropriate part of the book.

**Fourth step**

Ask yourself 'Do I want to do something about this problem?' If the answer is 'Yes' read through the *Brief Tips* section for each problem you have ticked.

**Fifth step**

Ask yourself 'Do I now want to find out more about these ideas for helping with the problem?' If the answer is 'Yes', turn to the pages to which you are referred in the Checklist. (If the answer is 'Yes — but later', move on to another **Problem Checklist** or the **Contents** to seek answers to your immediate questions).

**Sixth step**

Once you are reading the particular topic in the book, use the techniques in **The Importance of Asking Questions** to check whether you are understanding what you are reading, whether you could use the idea and whether you are concentrating on what you are doing.

### Seventh step

Once you have completed work on the topic, return to the **Checklists, Contents** or **Index,** and continue, using your questioning approach, to seek answers to your questions.

### HOW TO USE THIS BOOK: A Step-by-Step guide

### Start here

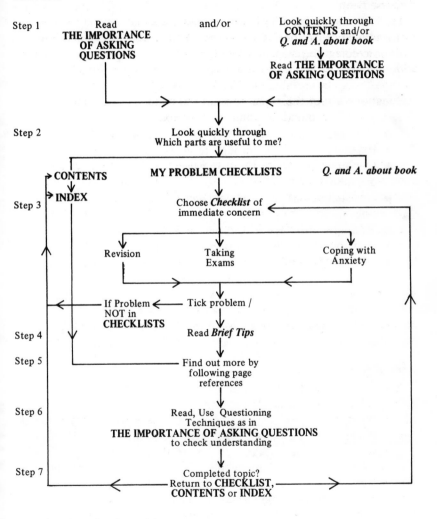

**Key** = Q. and A = Questions and Answers.

Emphasised line is the recommended sequence for the first use of the book.

I strongly recommend that you read through this book in exactly the same way I would recommend you to revise and take examinations — *with questions constantly in your mind.* Use these guidelines to develop your questioning techniques and then use them to *pick and choose the ideas which best seem to answer your questions.*

● Don't pick up this book after this moment without having a question in mind.

There are *two types of question* that I would recommend you ask yourself continuously. The first type is about *the topic you are studying* e.g. The First World War if you are studying History as a subject. The second type of question is about *you;* what you are doing and how you are proceeding when you are studying. *Both types of questions are of equal importance.*

### Questions about the topic you are studying

You can find questions about a topic you are studying from:—

● Old examination questions. These are usually obtainable from an Examining Board or through teachers, lecturers or libraries.
● Questions you have tried to answer during the course e.g. essay questions.
● Any suggestions or guidelines given to you by teachers, lecturers or tutors.
● Talking to friends and sharing ideas.
● Your own interests, the thing you want to know.
● The work you have studied during the year, indicated by headings in your notes. You can convert these topic headings into questions by using questions beginning with the six key words in the Kipling poem. i.e. What? When? Why? How? Where? Who?

   You would need to choose a topic and then see if you can think of a question beginning with any of those six words.

### An example

Using the History topic, The First World War, I constructed six questions.

> What .............................. were the main causes?
> When ................... was the turning point of the war?
> Why .................... were the casualties so enormous?
> How . was Germany made to pay at the end of the war?
> Where ...................... were the principal battlefields?
> Who .. were the politicians principally responsible for the war?

You will need to construct the same sort of topic questions in order to use this book. Some useful questions about this book and the topics within it would include:—

>What problems have I got with studying for exams?
>Why do I get so nervous and what can I do about it?
>How can reading this book solve my revision problems?
>Where should I revise?
>Who should I use to help me — and how?
>To what subjects do these ideas apply?
>How difficult would it be to try this idea?
>When should I start my revision?

## Questions about what you are doing, how you are proceeding

These are questions you ask yourself in order to keep a watchful eye on how you are spending your time; whether you know what you are doing and why you are doing it. Some useful questions to ask yourself when using this book would include:—

>What am I reading this page for?
>Why am I looking at this book?
>What do I want to find out?
>Where shall I look next?
>Have I understood what I have just read?
>When will I be justified in taking a break?
>Am I concentrating?
>What will I do immediately after I have finished this?
>What is the time?

You will notice that not all these questions have to begin with the six key words. It is the principle of questioning that is, and has been, so fundamental in learning for hundreds and, indeed, thousands of years e.g. Socrates was promoting the value of question and answer in ancient Greece (Socratic dialogue). The particular value of it has been expressed well by Rudyard Kipling in 'The Elephant's Child':—

>'I keep six honest serving-men
>They taught me all I knew
>Their names are What and Why and When
>And How and Where and Who'.

Q. *Who is the book written for?*

A. Anybody, of whatever age, who is taking examinations at any level — school tests and examinations, GCSE's and A Level, Scottish Highers, Certificates, Professional qualifications, Diplomas, first Degrees and Post Graduate qualifications. It is also written for anybody who wishes to help the student study most effectively, e.g. parents, teachers and friends. **Using Helpers** gives guidelines to both students and their helpers.

The ideas apply to any form of examinations — written or oral; word-based (descriptive); number-based (mathematical, problem solving) and multiple choice exams — taken in schools, colleges, Polytechnics and Universities. The basic principles involved in studying for all exams are the same.

Q. *What does it contain?*

A. It contains dozens of ideas on how, when, where, how much, with whom and what to *revise*; how to prepare yourself for *examinations*; what to do immediately before and during the exams themselves; and how to cope with any *anxiety* you feel. You can discover exactly what it contains by reading the **Contents; How to Use This Book: A Step-by-Step Guide; The Importance of Asking Questions;** the **Checklists** at the beginning of each section and the **Index.**

Q. *Have I got time to read it?*

A. Yes, definitely: Half an hour well spent in reading parts of this book is very likely to immediately *save you time.* One hour spent extracting ideas from the book will give you a very clear picture of what the book contains and enable you to put *effective ideas into practice immediately.* Thereafter, five, ten or fifteen minute periods of dipping into the book for particular ideas to cope with particular problems will probably be all you need.

Q. *Do I have to read the whole book?*

A. No. Select those parts that are relevant to your needs now and use them. You may never finish reading the book from cover-to-cover and that doesn't matter. Try, however, to form an outline idea of what is contained in the parts of the book you have not used. They may be useful later on. This book is designed to be *used,* not just read.

Q. *Where do the ideas come from?*

A. They come from hundreds of students I have worked with since 1970 when I began to work with individuals and groups of students to help them improve their studying. They come from my experience as a G.C.E. Ordinary Level examiner, in the past, and an Advanced Level examiner, in the present. They also come from the collective expertise of other authors of study skills, counselling and relaxation books and materials, whose work, wherever I have made direct use of it, is acknowledged. What little we know about how we learn from psychological research is also incorporated. Finally, the ideas come from teachers I have worked with both as colleagues and as a tutor on study skills courses for teachers.

Q. *Do the ideas work?*

A. Yes. Every one of the ideas contained in the book has worked for some student, somewhere. The vast majority have worked for large numbers of students. I also use them — and did so to write this book as I describe in **How did I write this book?**

Q. *Do I have to follow all these ideas?*

A. Definitely not. *There is no one perfect or correct way of revising or taking examinations.* There are numerous ideas that work. *Pick and choose* those ideas you feel would suit you and your needs. *Add them* to any ways you have for studying already that you want to retain.

It is worth noting that it is often difficult to change your old habits, your old ways of doing things. Even if they don't seem to work very well, at least they are known to you, familiar i.e. 'The devil you know rather than the devil you don't know'. My experience is that it is worth changing at least some of your old ways. It is likely you are already using some of the ideas in the book if you are studying effectively. If you are not using *any* of the ideas in this book, I'd be very surprised if you are studying effectively.

Bear in mind that new ideas often need a little practice. Sometimes, like any new skills, your peformance may be less effective for a very short time, before you see the real benefits. Having said that this may occur, the opposite is true of many of these ideas: you will see immediate improvement in performance.

Q. *If I've got the ability, do I need this book?*

A. You may not. Ability, hard work and determination have seen thousands of students successfully through the exam system — but not necessarily. I've explained why in **Why did I write this book?**

Q. *What makes this different from other books on studying for examinations?*

A. It is very comprehensive. It does not moralise and tell you what you *ought* to do or give you lots of 'good advice'. It is clear and straightforward to use. As it tells you how to use the book, it cuts down on the amount of time needed before you put the ideas into practice. Uniquely, it combines revision and examination techniques with ideas for coping with your whole lifestyle including any anxiety you may feel, to help you become a really efficient student.

Q.  *Why did I write this book?*

A.  I had personal needs in writing this book. Desiring a sense of achievement; to fulfil a creative need; to prove I could write a book by myself and financial reward (hopefully!) are four of them.

There were other very stongly felt reasons for writing this book, outlined below. They represent my philosophy of how we learn and our capability to do so.

- There are many useful and stimulating revision and examination techniques, although most students I meet are unfamiliar with them. I have collected them together in an easy-to-find and use form, as I have found other study skills books either rather daunting to use or lacking in detailed guidelines.

- 'How to Pass Exams without Anxiety' has developed from two sources: a booklet called 'How to Study for Exams' and the book 'Exams without Anxiety'. Readers' comments have encouraged me to produce this book, which incorporates their suggestions for improvement as well as the original materials. I have substantially expanded the original **Coping with Anxiety** and **Using Helpers** sections. I have included more ideas for improving revision and remembering as well as more examples of the ideas in practice.

- Most of us worry about examinations at some time in our lives. We may worry, for example, about how to revise, what to do in the exam room or how to stop our worrying getting out of control. The thirty or more ideas in the **Coping with Anxiety** section of the book are devised to help you in specific situations and at specific times during your revision and the examinations themselves.

- There is a belief that those who do well in examinations are those who have ability, work hard and are determined characters. Expressed as a sum, it would be
ABILITY + DETERMINATION + HARD WORK = ACHIEVEMENT

I would have difficulty in marking this sum, as I believe it is incomplete. Correct as it may be for many candidates, it is certainly inadequate as an explanation of the achievements of many others.

Two examples of this are:

— Those whose ability appears to produce achievement without hard work or determination. This is a category of candidate who is often referred to, but is, I suspect, less common than supposed. This candidate makes others feel sick!

— Those whose determination and hard work overcome their apparent lack of ability. In my first year of teaching I met a fourth year schoolboy who had a measured I.Q. of 71. He later successfully took Science 'O' levels, 'A' level Chemistry and went on to Higher Education. As at the time it was supposedly a borderline decision as to whether he went to a special school or not, this *both* demonstrated to me the value of absorbing interest, hard work and determination *and* commented upon the value of summarising a human being's ability to learn, by a number.

I believe that *Achievement* is not the sum of three but *five factors*. They are:—

(1)   *Ability*

Whilst there are obvious limits to an individual's ability to achieve in particular areas of activity, I believe that much ability of the most able to the least able, remains untapped and underdeveloped. Further, I believe most candidates can considerably improve their performance in examinations and that the vast majority who are entered for a particular exam have, at the very least, the ability to *pass* it. With better *technique,* most candidates whose 'O' level or 'A' level work I mark, would be gaining more marks.

(2)   *Determination*

Determination is a very useful trait, if it is channelled and focussed in the appropriate direction. I have met very determined people who have striven in entirely inappropriate ways and as a result exhausted themselves and marred their exam performance.

(3)   *Work rate*

I've met large numbers of candidates who have worked very hard but inefficiently and whose performance in examinations has been a suprise and disappointment both to themselves and their teachers, families and friends. Hard work should bring achievement when coupled with efficient and appropriate revision and exam techniques. Indeed most students should be able to achieve satisfactory standards without *hard* work, if their techniques are good.

(4)   *Techniques*

Here I am referring to the contents of this book.

(5)    *Coping with yourself as a person*
    Success in examinations is not just a matter of using your thinking or intellectual ability. It is also dependent upon your feelings and behaviour. In particular how you cope with the potentially bewildering tasks you aim to complete; how you cope with any past experiences of learning and taking exams (frequently negative); how you cope with your own or other people's expectations and how you cope with any anxiety you experience, are often just as important as ability. This is the reason for a Coping with Anxiety section being incorporated with Revision and Examination Techniques in this book.
    My revised sum would be:—

ABILITY + DETERMINATION + WORKRATE + TECHNIQUE + COPING WITH YOURSELF = ACHIEVEMENT

● These techniques guidelines will be useful for all studying. The four techniques which occur throughout:—
    questioning,
    summarising,
    task setting and
    time allocating,
coupled with the approaches for coping with anxiety are a means of enjoying and succeeding in learning in almost every aspect of your life.

Q.   **How did I write this book?**
A.   I used many of the ideas in this book in writing it. They are arranged in approximate order of use in the question mark opposite, although many were used very frequently throughout e.g. questioning and key word revision cards.

The question mark shape is made up of the following steps, reading clockwise from the lower left:

STARTED HERE
ASKED QUESTIONS
WHAT WORKS BEST?
READ, WATCHED
LISTENED
TRIED IDEAS IN GROUPS
TRIED IDEAS FOR ME
ASKED MORE QUESTIONS
REFINED IDEAS
WROTE DOWN IDEAS
WROTE INDIVIDUAL PAGES OF NOTES
TRIED THE NOTES OUT
EVALUATED EFFECTIVENESS
ASSEMBLED NOTES INTO A4 PAGES
FILED NOTES IN WALLET FOLDERS
USED CREATIVE PATTERNS
ASSEMBLED FIRST DRAFT
USED HELPERS
NOTED FEEDBACK
REWROTE NOTES
DEVELOPED STANDARDISED FORMAT
SET TIME LIMITS
VARIED TASKS/TOPICS
HOLIDAY BREAK
WROTE IN SHORT BURSTS
SET DEADLINES
SWAM AND PLAYED POOL
TICKED OFF PROGRESS ON WALLCHART. USED COLOURS
LISTENED TO MOZART AND PAUL SIMON
REVISED DEADLINE
WORKED REGULARLY
FINISHED HERE

EXAMS WITHOUT ANXIETY

# 2
# Revision

| I have/may have problems with:— | Tick if it applies to you ✓ | Brief Tips | Where to find out more (pp.) |
|---|---|---|---|
| Getting started with revision | | Make a list of what you have got to do subject by subject. Use the system suggested in this book | 21-26 |
| Deciding when I should start revising | | Now. It's never too early to start and you can revise until close to the exams. | 33-35 |
| Remembering facts | | Ask lots of questions and as soon as you know the answers e.g. from reading notes, test yourself at once, *without* looking at the notes. | 44-47 |
| Understanding what I am revising | | Ask yourself questions about what you are doing; know what you are revising and why. | 10,11 44 |
| Remembering what I have already revised | | Take brief notes on cards on the topics you have revised. Use these cards to test yourself a few times, for a few minutes a time, before the exam. | 39-42 |
| Leaving my revision too late | | Try doing a small piece of revision on a topic that interests you *now* — thirty mins. may be enough. Nibble away at the revision. | 33-35 |
| Revising by myself | | Know what you are doing (see *What should I revise?*) Could you and a friend help each other? | 21- 26 106-110 |
| Making a revision timetable that *works* | | Have a trial period of a week or two to get it right. Be flexible. | 33, 36 |
| Knowing the best way to revise | | See *How to revise*. It is essential to recall what you have just tried to learn *immediately*. | 38-43 |
| How to use my notes and/or books for revision | | Use your notes if you know they are good enough. Improve them and reorganise them if they are not. | 27-28 |
| The order in which to revise subjects or topics | | See *What Should I revise?* Vary subjects and topics to keep your interest going. | 21-26 |
| Knowing which topics to revise | | See *What Should I revise?* Know your strengths and weaknesses. Look at old exam papers. Speak to people who can guide you. | 21-26 10-11 51-52 |
| Revising mathematics and other number-based subjects | | Practice answering questions without books giving you answers. Time yourself for exam length answers. | 47 |
| Whether to revise all topics or to ignore some | | You can't usually revise *all* topics equally well. Most people like to cover at least 70%. | 21-26 |
| Concentrating | | See *How can I improve my concentration?* Make sure you've got a good place to revise. | 29-33 |
| Making enough time for revision | | Although there is never enough time and you need breaks, time off and relaxation, planning a revision timetable will help. | 33-37 |
| Finding a good place to revise | | Find a place where you like to be and which has a good feel to it. | 30-31 |
| Deciding how many hours a day or week to revise | | Make a weekly timetable. This can help decide the number of hours you revise. This will vary from 15 to 40 hours a week of private study. Set yourself daily targets. | 32-37 |
| Whether to take time off for relaxation and a social life | | Take short breaks and at least a day a week and an evening or two off. | 33-37 73-74, 86-87 |

## Introduction

Much revision is misnamed as many students find themselves trying to learn and memorise topics for the first time when they start to revise. Although the revise-as-you-go technique described in **Key word revision cards** is an effective way to revise and although most revision begins some weeks before the exams, you can learn these new topics efficiently if you use the appropriate ideas contained in this section of the book.

## Efficient Revision

Efficient revision replaces shallow learning with learning in some depth; replaces bewilderment with confidence; replaces the myth of a few fortunate people with photographic memories with the realisation that *you* can use your visual memory to aid recall; and replaces the common — and useless — feeling of guilt with a structured revision programme.

*The features of efficient revision* are that you:—

(1) set yourself a *clear and specific target*.

(2) *set a time scale* for each task. Not 'I must do it', but 'I must do it by X time'.

(3) pick *a task which is sufficiently demanding* i.e. that is neither too easy nor too difficult at that moment.

(4) can *verify your success* in learning the topic both to yourself (by testing yourself in some way) or to others (by using them as testers, for example).

(5) have *a feeling of accomplishment* after completing the task.

Thus features of efficient revision are *planning your revision, organising revision time,* knowing *how to revise* and *memorising techniques* and each of these is considered in turn.

(1) *Developing a complete picture* of what you might be examined on in a particular subject will help you decide what to revise and with which topic to begin your revision. Using the suggestions below will prevent this from being overwhelming.

(2) You can develop this whole picture by consulting *a syllabus* for the course. If you have, as is quite common, never seen one, your subject teacher is likely to have one and libraries in schools (sometimes) and colleges, Polytechnics and Universities (usually) keep copies. It may not be necessary to find the syllabus however. Many internal examinations i.e. exams set and marked within the school or college, are based upon the work you have actually been presented with during the year. Thus, the main topic and sub-topic headings from your notes or handouts from teachers and lecturers can give you quite a complete picture. Questions you have been answering and emphasis given to particular topics can give further guidelines.

*It is advisable* that you check with teachers and lecturers about the scope of the examination (and use any guidelines you obtain from them).

(3) You will find anxiety you feel about 'covering the syllabus' is reduced if you are clear and specific about what you are revising, why you are revising it and how it fits into the overall revision of that subject. One way of deciding this is to *take a separate sheet of paper for each subject* you are studying and write on it the *principal topics* and *sub-topics* that you have studied on the course leading to the examination. For some subjects you may need a second sheet of paper. Arrange the topics and sub-topics in columns, allowing 4 or 6 cm space between each column.

To clarify terminology in the example (p.24) 'Geography' is the subject, 'National Parks' is a topic and 'Homes in National Parks' is a sub-topic.

### Subjects, Topics and Symbols

Once you have listed the principal topics and sub-topics for each subject, you can use this simple symbol system to indicate the amount of interest, understanding/knowledge, ease or difficulty, urgency and usefulness of each.

### When completing it:

- You don't *have* to use a symbol from each of these five sections above. Thus, if *usefulness* does not seem relevant to a particular topic, then do not write that symbol next to it.
- You can invent your own symbols if you'd prefer; there's nothing magic about these.

| | | |
|---|---|---|
| How much<br>*INTEREST*<br>do you have in it? | ⟨✓✓✓⟩<br>✓✓<br>✓<br>(✗) | Very interested<br>Quite interested<br>A bit interested<br>Not interested |
| How much<br>*UNDERSTANDING AND*<br>*KNOWLEDGE* do you have of<br>it? | ⟨OKAY⟩<br>OK<br>?<br>⟨??⟩ | Clearly know/understand it<br>Know it/understand it quite well<br>Understand/know a bit but<br>probably not enough for *pass*<br>answer standard<br>Don't know it/understand it at all |
| How<br>*EASY OR DIFFICULT*<br>do you find it? | ⟨EASY⟩<br>EASY<br>DIFF<br>⟨DIFF⟩ | Easy to do/understand<br>Quite easy to do/understand<br>Quite difficult to understand<br>Most difficult to understand |
| How *SOON* is the exam;<br>how much *TIME* do you have? | ⟨!!!⟩<br>!!<br>!<br>◯ | Very soon; little time<br>Soon; some time<br>Quite soon; a bit more time<br>Some way off; most time |
| How *USEFUL* is it?<br>For example, how likely is it<br>to come up in the exam? How<br>useful is it for other topics or<br>subjects? Can you use it in your<br>everyday life? | ⟨✹ ✹ ✹⟩<br>✹ ✹<br>✹<br>⊕ | Essential<br>Useful<br>Of some use<br>Of no use |

## Deciding priorities

Using the symbol system can help you decide your priorities. As a general rule, you will find it easier to start your revision where you have recorded the most positive symbols in the Interest, Understanding and Knowledge, Ease and Usefulness categories. (Urgency is obviously important, but usually needs further specifying. This is assisted by focussing on the other four categories. Where time is short the examination timetable will help you determine urgency.)

The first two symbols are the most positive viz:—

INTEREST
UNDERSTANDING/KNOWLEDGE
EASE/DIFFICULTY
USEFULNESS

Look in particular for circled symbols, both positive and negative. *Circled positive symbols are a good starting point*, particularly if there are two or more together. This is particularly the case if you are finding it difficult to get started on your revision or your concentration has been poor. It will help your confidence to tackle a topic at which there is a high probability you will succeed. The second most positive symbol also represents topics that you are likely to be able to revise competently at an early stage.

You are probably going to find it more difficult to learn and immediately recall those *circled negative symbols*, particularly if you only have a short time left in which to revise.

## What should I revise and in what order?
## An example

Kate, aged 15, has listed some principal topics on her 4th Year Geography syllabus. Next to each topic she has written symbols to reflect her *interest, understanding/knowledge* and *the ease or difficulty* she finds in each. Later she describes how she uses it to decide what to revise and in what order.

<u>Geography Revision</u>

<u>DARTMOOR</u>
1. Types of Landscape · √√√ OK (EASY)
2. Granite and Tors · √√√ OK (EASY)
3. Landscape Weathering · √√ OK EASY
4. Relief and Temperature · √ OK EASY
5. Dartmoor Traffic Flow · √ OK EASY

<u>National Parks</u>
1. Position of all National Parks in UK · √ ? EASY
2. Dartmoor as a National Park · √√ ? EASY
3. Homes in National Parks · √ ? EASY
4. Conflicting Interests in National Parks · √ ? EASY

<u>Blackton Manor Farm</u>
1. System farming on a farm · √ OK EASY
2. Map of Uses on farm · √ ? DIFF

<u>PHYSICAL FACTORS IN FARMING</u>
1. Systems · √ ? EASY
2. Middlefell farm Langdale · √√ ? EASY
3. How do Soils affect farming · √ ? EASY

<u>Von Thünen</u>
1. Cost of Transport · √√ OK EASY
2. Graphs · √ OK EASY
3. Distance from Farm, Affect Land use · √ OK EASY

<u>Land use around a Town</u>
1. Monoton · √ ? EASY
2. Sampling Graphs · √√ OK EASY
3. Anomalies · √√ OK EASY
4. Scatter Diagrams · √√ OK EASY

<u>Hill Farming</u>
1. The Effect of Slope on Farming · √ ? EASY
2. Income each Year · √√ OK EASY
3. Significance · √ ? DIFF
4. Trelowcth Manor Farm · √ ? DIFF

<u>Farmers Land Use Decision Making</u>
1. Diagram · √√ OK EASY
2. Ability to See need for Change · √√ OK EASY
3. Reason for Farming · √ OK EASY
4. Reasons for Farming · √√ OK (EASY)
5. A Herefordshire Farm · √√ OK EASY

<u>Stages in the Development of Agriculture</u>
1. Hunting and Gathering · √√ OK EASY
2. Subsistence Farming · √√ OK EASY
3. Peasant Farming · √√ OK EASY
4. Commercial Farming · √√ OK EASY
5. Major world Farming Patterns · √ ? DIFF

- You can mix in some topics with the more negative symbols in between those topics with more positive symbols, as your revision progresses and your confidence grows.

- Some people like to tackle some difficult topic first. They may feel by doing so that they have set themselves a positive challenge or challenged their fear. There is no *correct* order. Choose the order that meets your needs.

**In the example,** Kate said

'I will start by revising the work which I found most difficult and the work which I did earlier in the course. I will do this because when I sit down ready to revise I am at my most alert and my concentration is good.

By looking at the list I made for revising, I will mix in *early topics* I did, e.g. 'Types of Landscape', 'Granite Tors', with topics which I found difficult, e.g. 'Significance of Hill Farming' and 'Major world farming patterns'.

I will revise last the subjects I found easy, e.g. 'Reasons for Farming' and those that are fresh in my mind, e.g. 'Hunting and Gathering', Subsistence Farming'. I already understand these quite well and they will not take long to learn when I come to finishing off my revision'.

Kate's choice of order for topic revision feels correct to her. It is a subject in which she has a fair degree of confidence: a fact reflected by the large number of positive symbols on the page. This confidence enables her to start her revision with some *relatively* difficult topics. If the page had been covered with negative symbols, it would probably have been the best confidence-building plan to start with a few positive symbols.

## Spotting examination questions

*Question spotting* is a risky business. Given that an examiner could ask many different questions about a particular topic, trying to guess a particular question is obviously difficult. In many subjects a core of topics are going to appear, with some variation from year to year, e.g. a topic appearing in three or four years of a five year period. In some examination papers there is some reasonably sure 'banker' question. Examinations which are set and marked *internally* i.e. within the school or college, are going to concentrate on the actual topics which the teacher or lecturer has presented to groups during the course. It is likely that *topic spotting* is more reliable in these exams, whereas in *externally* set and marked examinations, e.g. most GCSE and Advanced level subjects, the emphasis of the questions will be to reflect the work of many students and their teachers. Different emphasis is likely to be given to topics in separate schools and colleges. GCSE includes internal and external assessment.

There is no substitute for extra work if you want to be certain of being able to answer the number of questions required. One effective way of preparing is to **Devise questions around a topic,** another to **List useful definitions.**

### Devise questions around a topic

By practising asking questions about a particular topic you can increase your flexibility and preparedness for the examination itself. *List* past exam questions, grouping them into *types* of question and according to *emphasis* they may have in common. Add to these any questions you have been asked during your course and any that you and others could make up to give other angles on the topic. Check to see which questions occur most frequently on past papers, as one rough guide to the likelihood of particular questions occurring.

### List useful definitions

Make lists of definitions of the *key words, ideas or concepts* that you may need to use in the examination. Learn these as part of your revision.

The following ideas can help you plan your revision.

**Build up good notes from which to revise**

Organise and, if necessary, re-organise your notes by

(1) Keeping all your notes, essays, reports and other material on a particular *topic* together. As the studying year proceeds it is often unnecessary for material to be separated because of the date you completed it or the type of material.

(2) Grouping related topics together for ease of revision: related topics can be revised together.

(3) Discussing your notes with others. Criticise them and, where appropriate, re-write parts of them.

(4) Reducing your bulky notes to key words and key ideas as explained in **Key word revsion cards.** Use these cards for the major part of your revision, cross-referencing them with your original notes.

(5) Drawing together brief summaries of topics and sub-topics in a visually creative way. One method is to use simple *spider diagrams* to help you remember the main points of a topic. Each leg of the spider can be a different colour to help you differentiate between them, associating a colour and a piece of information. The number of legs your spider possesses will vary! These can be easily and quickly reproduced at the beginning of an exam.

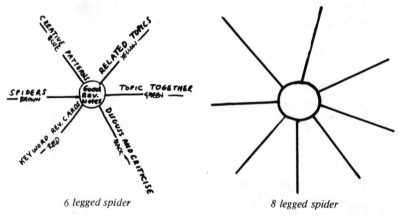

6 legged spider        8 legged spider

(6) *Patterned notes* are another way of summarising your understanding and finding links and associations between information and ideas.

Usually when students make notes they try to force their ideas into a linear (straight line) structure e.g.

    (1)

    (2)

    (3)

This often creates problems when they think of a new idea that does not fit into the structure. Alternatively, dissatisfaction with the order of the items, or remembering another item and having no space in which to add it can lead. to several re-writes and re-orderings.

Patterned notes help to overcome this problem. They can be used creatively to allow the mind to associate freely (they are sometimes called **creative brain patterns**). They can also be used for summarising very quickly what you have just been revising. In 5 minutes, using this system, you can recall a complete topic on paper or card.

You start patterned notes in the centre of a sheet of paper. Your subsequent ideas can spray out around it. When you are using it creatively, don't attempt to evaluate your ideas, just write them down. When all your thoughts on the topic are down on paper then you can evaluate the ideas and decide which order you will put them in. By this method you are trying to separate the creative and evaluative processes of the mind. You can use colours to group information and ideas together and add numbers to indicate which ideas are most important or the order in which you would answer a question. Make your notes as brief as possible. They are just for you and don't have to make sense to anyone else.

Some best times to use patterned notes are: when you are about to start writing a piece of work, e.g. as an outline answer to a question in the examination; when you want to check your recall of the topic you have just revised; when you want to summarise some longer notes; in planning an essay or the answer to any coursework question; as a facing or front page to your more conventional notes i.e. you can use the two forms of notes alongside each other. Experiment and find out when you find them most useful. More information about this approach can be found in Tony Buzan's book 'Use Your Head'.

*An example of patterned notes,* summarising this information follows.

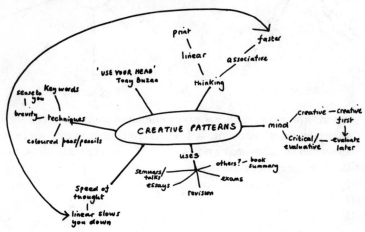

## Have an overview of what you have to revise

**Deciding what to revise** offers suggestions on how to do this. This will help you decide *how much to revise* and in what order. How much of a subject to revise is a difficult issue. For the majority of examinations you can be very successful without attempting to revise 100% of the syllabus. There are some examinations for some professional groups that demand very high levels or perfect knowledge about certain key areas, e.g. for doctors, accountants and lawyers. The majority of examinations and examiners do not expect the whole syllabus to be 'covered'. Obviously, the more you cover in your revision the more chances you have of finding questions you can answer. However, this will still depend on how carefully you have checked with your teachers, syllabus and examinations and which topics you have revised, e.g. it would be possible to miss a topic which is compulsory and worth more marks than other topics. **Know your examinations** and you will maximise the chances of your finding questions you can answer.

My guess — and it is only a guess, with the provisos mentioned already — is that covering 70% of a typical syllabus during revision would provide a good chance of finding enough questions to answer. As I consider this to be the least reliable guideline in this book, I would *strongly recommend you seek the guidance of others,* teachers and lecturers for each subject you take if you are concerned about this issue.

## Keep a diary or note book

There are several uses for these.

(1) You can use this to monitor your progress, commenting on how well you are progressing and noting points of which you wish to be reminded.

(2) To note down ideas and information as they occur. These can be transferred later to revision cards or notes.

(3) To plan the next day's work on the evening before.

You may find other uses for them. You may also wish to carry blank postcards around with you for noting down the same sort of information, as an alternative or in addition to a diary or notebook.

## Vary subjects, topics and methods throughout your revision

Vary these each week and each day. You will find that you are more likely to sustain your concentration by doing so. At the same time, mix the difficulty of the topics revised, using the confidence gained from one piece of work successfully completed to help you tackle a slightly more difficult topic.

The following are features of helpful work environments.

(1)   The key feature of where to revise is that you seek for yourself a place where you like to be and where it is easiest to work. It must have *a good feel to it:* a kitchen table (where I am writing now); lying on your bed; at a desk, in an armchair, can all have this feel.

(2)   It is advisable to work some of the time at a desk, to prepare yourself for exam conditions, particularly closer to the exams.

(3)   A clear desk or table top, with enough space to have materials assembled and accessible around you. This will reduce time wasting and delaying tactics!

(4)   Your area of a room should be well lit (a table lamp may help), well ventilated and warm enough to be comfortable without causing you to feel drowsy. It should also ensure you have the minimum unwanted interruptions and distractions.

(5)   A pleasant, non-distracting view can aid concentration. As I write I have a wall in front of me. It is light coloured and I can see two pictures I like and a chart on which I am ticking off my progress in writing this book. Soon I will be ticking off **Where to revise.** A pin board or wall chart in front of you can be very useful to plan and record your progress.

(6)   There is a lot of debate and argument in homes about whether you need to be working in a quiet environment. I don't believe there is *one* answer to this issue. If you, as the student, feel the need for quiet then it is important. If, on the other hand, listening to the radio, tapes or records aids your work, then continue to do so.

Television is another dimension, for the visual image is powerful and watching television requires the use of two major senses. I can only listen to television when I am working, not watch and listen. Both can be used to advantage, by helping you relax and/or associating some sound or vision with a particular revision topic.

*The essential point is to be honest with yourself.* Is the environment you've created really helping your study — or acting, to some degree at least, as a substitute for work?

*Away from your ideal revision environment* you may have problems in applying yourself to revision.

You may find it easier to apply yourself if you plan to work in short bursts, being highly specific about what you are going to do, e.g. summarise two pages of notes onto a revision card; reorganise your notes on a topic; write an outline answer to a question. Being highly specific about such tasks can give you a good chance of completing them before being interrupted by friends or going for something to eat or drink.

Make the effort to find your *next best work places* in school, college or home.

These may be a study cubicle in a public library, a quieter corner of a school or college library (if it exists!), an empty classroom, an armchair in front of the television.

Finally, you can *vary where you study occasionally*. Working at a friend's home is one example. Such variety may also help you adjust to taking examinations in different rooms at a later stage.

Improving concentration is frequently *either* a matter of using more effective study approaches *or* resolving a personal concern which is interfering with your study. In the latter case, talking to someone may help, e.g. a friend, a relative, a teacher, doctor or counsellor, as described in **Using Helpers.**

The following study approaches will aid your concentration:—

(1) *Find a place to work which has a good feel to it.* It should be a place that has enough light, heat and space around for books and papers. It should be a place you like to be.

(2) *Have all materials you need assembled around you* from the start. Don't give yourself an excuse to postpone starting.

(3) *Devise questions* to which you seek answers, as described in **The Importance of Asking Questions.**

(4) *Be active in what you do,* e.g. speak aloud, tape record, talk to someone, write notes.

(5) *Pick topics* to study which you already *understand,* find most *easy to tackle and* are of most *interest* or use to you as well as those which are particularly *useful* or *urgent.* Specific ideas are given in **What Should I Revise?**

(6) *Set yourself realistic small targets.* This will give you more chance to succeed in reaching your goal. Success will increase both your self confidence and your work rate.

(7) *Vary* both the topics you study and the methods you use.

(8) *Study for short periods of time*, at least initially. 15, 20, 25 and 30 mins. can be very effectively used on routine study. Short breaks can be used constructively either for relaxation or recalling what you have been doing.

(9) *Rest and relax.* Be positive about your breaks from study. Give yourself a day off a week at least and other free time when you are not obliged to feel guilty. A drink or a favourite television programme can be used as a reward for the completion of a specific revision unit. Physical exercise, e.g. a walk, a run, a swim, yoga exercises or team games can help revitalise you, much studying is relatively passive.

(10) *Check your sleep.* Lack of concentration is often due to failing to look after a basic need for sleep. **Getting to sleep at night** offers several ideas to help those with this difficulty.

13 ideas to help you organise time.

(1) *Make a revision timetable* day-by-day from now until the examinations begin *and* for the period between examinations. The problem with revision timetables is that they often go wrong after the first day: to counteract this:—

— Have a two week or one week *trial period* to enable you to determine what tasks you can realistically complete in a day.
— Be flexible e.g. different *subject* headings for each day will enable you to vary the *topics* you revise.

*An example of a revision timetable* is included.

(2) *Pin up your timetable* or time plan on a wall in a prominent place e.g. above your table or desk. Coloured pens can make it clear and attractive.

(3) *Revise as you go* : start weeks before the exams. If you haven't started before reading this, start now. It's never too early to start and you can still revise until very close to your examinations. Starting 6 to 8 weeks before the exam is a typical revision period for most students.

(4) *Include in your revision* timetable any *unfinished work* you still have to do as part of your year's studies. You do not have to complete this work *before* starting revision. You can revise this subject work as soon as it is completed, so it can become part of your revision.

(5) *Know how you use the 168 hours in the week*. You can use the **Time Chart** to calculate exactly how you have used the time in one week and record hours in these categories, below. Alternatively, you can do a rough calculation and complete the table below. You have been provided with a daily and weekly column; complete either or both according to which you find easier.

(6) *Set yourself a daily target of revision hours.*
An alternative to a large scale or weekly revision timetable is to set yourself a daily target of revision hours e.g. 4 hours a day. This time unit can be shown on a chart marked off in quarter hour units with your favourite colours, to show you effective and concentrated use of time. You could use this idea by itself or alongside marking off topics you have revised on a chart.

Angela, a final year undergraduate, combined this with positive self statements ('It's really working', 'I've 40 whole days left') to successfully complete her revision. She monitored the quarter hour units on a chart and felt a sense of achievement and optimism: there are a great many quarter hours in 4 hours revision a day for 40 days!

(7) *Working late at night*
As explained in **Getting to Sleep at Night** there are wide differences in people's ability to work effectively late at night or the early hours of the morning. For a typical student 3 or 4 hours work in an evening is likely to be as much as they can effectively tackle. It would certainly not be advisable to work very late or long the night before an exam. On other nights, developing the effective self-monitoring this book is encouraging, will enable you to decide whether you are working efficiently.

(8) *For routine revision,* you can *work in short periods of time* i.e. as short as 20-30 mins. Some topics and subjects call for longer periods but numerous sub-topics can be revised in this way. Mathematical, Scientific or problem based revision will often require longer periods e.g. 1 hour, to follow through a sequence of techniques and knowledge.

(9) It is important to *set a time limit on completing a task* i.e. 'I will do X by . . .'

**TIME CHART**

| | Total hours Daily | Weekly |
|---|---|---|
| Sleeping, dressing, washing, etc. | ——— | ——— |
| Travel | ——— | ——— |
| Classes, laboratories, etc. | ——— | ——— |
| Going out socially | ——— | ——— |
| Recreation and exercise | ——— | ——— |
| Watching television | ——— | ——— |
| Eating | ——— | ——— |
| Domestic responsibilities and tasks | ——— | ——— |
| Totals | ——— | ——— |
| Hours remaining in the day/week that may be used for private study | ——— | ——— |
| | (Total subtracted from 24 hrs.) | (Total subtracted from 168 hrs). |

(10) *Reward yourself* by taking *breaks* of at least a few minutes between work spells. You can take longer breaks for a drink or to watch a favourite TV programme. Breaks can also be used for actively recalling what you have just been trying to learn.

(11) *Divide the week into 21 sessions*

Another way of organising your time is to see the week as seven mornings, seven afternoons and seven evenings. Think of each session as a maximum of 3 hours long. Plan to work, formally in school or college or privately, around 15 sessions, giving a maximum working week of 45 hours out of the 168 hours in the week.

Using this system, ensure you take about 6 sessions for relaxation, entertainment and as a complete break from study.

(12) *The number of hours a week to revise* will vary widely according to what level of examinations you are studying, how many subjects you are taking and the amount of formal study, e.g. classes, lectures you are continuing to attend. However, private revising time close to the examinations is likely to be a minimum of 15 hours a week and a maximum of around 40 hours a week.

(13) *A very important rule of thumb*

For *every one unit of time* e.g. half an hour *you give to reading* i.e. trying to take in or assimilate information you should spend *at least the same amount of time on* trying to *recall* what you have just read.

It is by *recalling* that we *remember* what we have *read* (heard or seen). *So, the order is:—*

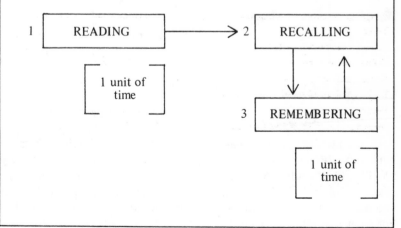

The first week of this timetable is complete in some detail: other weeks can be completed in the same way. If you are continuing to attend full time education during the day, the evenings or weekends will become more important and can be sub-divided into smaller units, if necessary.

| DAYS OF THE MONTH OF: | MON | TUES | WED | THURS | FRI | SAT | SUN |
|---|---|---|---|---|---|---|---|
| (Month) | 7 | 8 | 9 | 10 | 11 | 12 | 13 |
| a.m. | Subject A | Subject C | Voluntary work | Subject D | WHOLE DAY | Subject E | Subject E |
| p.m. | Walk Squash Coffee-friend | Shopping | Subjects B and C | Subjects B and C | VISIT TO | Review of ABCD | TV Friend's home |
| Evening | Subject B (2 topics) | Subject A (1 topic) | Subject C | Subject B | TOWN | Meet friend at DISCO | Review cards Plan next week |
| | 14 | 15 | 16 | 17 | 18 | 19 | 20 |
| a.m. | | | | | | | |
| p.m. | | | | | | | |
| Evening | | | | | | | |
| | 21 | 22 | 23 | 24 | 25 | 26 | 27 |
| a.m. | | | | | | | |
| p.m. | | | | | | | |
| Evening | | | | | | | |
| | 28 | 29 | 30 | 31 | 1 | 2 | 3 |
| a.m. | | | | | | | |
| p.m. | | | | | | | |
| Evening | | | | | | | |
| | 4 | 5 | 6 | 7 | 8 | 9 | 10 |
| a.m. | | | | | | | |
| p.m. | | | | | | | |
| Evening | | | | | | | |

Time already committed during the Examination and Revision period e.g. social events, classes, exams.

Time that may be available for revision: you would fill in subjects or topics in these spaces.

If you have difficulty in making time to revise or in finding a balance between revision and other activities, completing this time chart may help you identify the hours when it will be most effective to revise. Fill in the spaces in this daily record at the end of each day indicating exactly what you did each hour period. It is important that you record what you did, not what you intended to do.

| HOURS | MON | TUES | WED | THURS | FRI | SAT | SUN |
|---|---|---|---|---|---|---|---|
| a.m. 12- 5 | | | | | | | |
| 5- 6 | | | | | | | |
| 6- 7 | | | | | | | |
| 7- 8 | | | | | | | |
| 8- 9 | | | | | | | |
| 9-10 | | | | | | | |
| 10-11 | | | | | | | |
| 11-12 | | | | | | | |
| p.m.12- 1 | | | | | | | |
| 1- 2 | | | | | | | |
| 2- 3 | | | | | | | |
| 3- 4 | | | | | | | |
| 4- 5 | | | | | | | |
| 5- 6 | | | | | | | |
| 6- 7 | | | | | | | |
| 7- 8 | | | | | | | |
| 8- 9 | | | | | | | |
| 9-10 | | | | | | | |
| 10-11 | | | | | | | |
| 11-12 | | | | | | | |

*   If you are attending full-time education during the day, you may find it more useful to record half hour units in the late afternoon and evening, as well as in free time and lunch-times during the day.

In order to revise efficiently, you can draw upon a wide range of ideas about how we learn. These have been grouped together in **Memorising** and are relevant to all subjects at whatever level. Additionally, specific ideas are included to help those studying **Mathematically based subjects, Science and Technology.** These are preceded by a description of a reliable **Basic Revision method** and the suggestion of a **Key word revision card** system.

- A key theme in all these approaches is to make the most ACTIVE use of as many of your SENSES as possible. In particular, for you to make the best use of your *visual* (sight) and *aural* (sound) memory. Some people are more inclined to remember visually, some aurally. It will help you to know your own best style and most powerful sense, which you can discover by trying the ideas in **Memorising**. It is also absolutely essential to *actively recall* what you have just been doing; as in **A Basic Revision Method** and **Key word revision cards.**

- In contrast to this, the *Commonest Revision fault* is to *sit passively with book or notes open in front of you for hours,* attempting to read and 'take it all in'. Frequently, the results are poor; you do not remember most of what you were reading; long periods are spent over the same page whilst feeling increasingly disheartened.

This basic revision method uses a number of different learning ideas in combination. It is very *active;* it involves *repetition* and *testing yourself;* it ensures you *minimise mistakes;* it involves using your *visual* and *aural* memory; it breaks down learning into *manageable parts* and ensures you are recalling *recent* learning.

If it is coupled with the **Key word revision cards** idea, you add to these *concise, manageable summaries; colour and design* to stimulate visual memory and *frequent use* in very short bursts of time to ensure continued recall and memory.

This is a basic method for most routine descriptive (word based) revision and some problem solving, mathematical revision, involving either four or five steps

## *Step One*

Read your notes and seek answers to questions, as described in **The Importance of Asking Questions.**

Be as active in your reading as possible e.g. talk to yourself, walk around the room (even though people may give you funny looks). Speak into a tape recorder.

## *Step two*

When you feel you have understood and can remember what you have read, *close up your notes.*

## *Step three*

Now actively recall what you've just been reading, asking again the same questions *without* looking at your notes, until you have exhausted your recall of the whole topic you've been revising. Whilst doing so write down what you have recalled in *brief notes on a card* or *a sheet of paper.* It may help you to have the questions written down to refer to in the recalling process.

## *Step four*

*Check* the original notes with the new ones. Have you recalled all the answers to the questions you were asking?

*If yes,* you have created a *master card,* which you can use to re-revise without having to consult the original lengthier notes.

*If no,*

## *Step five*

Re-read your original notes as in Step one above, looking particularly for those points you originally missed. Repeat Steps 2 to 4 above, writing out *all* the points again, not just those missed the first time: by doing so, you will still be treating the topic as a whole and improving your recall of the *whole* topic.

This may appear time consuming and cumbersome but it is not. It ensures a high degree of recall which reading a lot of notes does not.

# Key word revision cards

Key word revision cards are a popular and effective way of developing your revision notes. The object is to write (or draw) *brief outline notes* immediately after you have completed work on a topic. Your intention is to record the minimum number of words to retain a full understanding of the information the next time you look at, and use, the card. These words — the *key* words, are designed to stimulate your recall of the topic without the necessity to write complete sentences or continuous prose. Cards can also be used for recording, and recalling, *diagramatic data, cross-sectional drawings, graphs, tables or formula.*

**Starting your cards**

You can start making these cards at any time, not just at those times, closer to exams, which you think of as revision times. Immediately you have completed a piece of homework or coursework you could summarise it onto a card, which as well as being a preparation for revision will become a part of revision. If you read an interesting article, see a relevant television programme or find a useful section in a book, brief outline notes on a card can quickly capture the moment.

The cards will quickly build up and can be grouped in subject/topic groups. They can be kept in boxes, plastic wallets and/or be held together with elastic bands.

Cards can be of any size. The three most popular sizes are A5, postcard size and a size somewhat smaller than postcard size. Postcard size tends to be the most popular as you can condense a considerable amount of information on to it and it is very convenient to carry in pocket or bag. Cards have advantages over paper in that they are more durable. A further advantage is that they help you develop confidence in your ability to manage the volume of revision you are required to tackle. Revising from a series of small, non-bulky cards seems so much more manageable than overwhelming piles of A4 notes in files or ring binders. You can always consult your main notes if a point on your card is unclear, amending your card as you do so. Cards are easy to read on a bus; in a common room; waiting in a corridor or during a lunchtime or break from classes.

**Advantages of using your own cards**

There is nothing new about a card system like this. Commercially produced cards on particular subjects have become a growth industry over the last decade or two e.g. 'Key Facts' cards and their rivals. *Making your own can produce better notes for revision.* This is because you can:—
● Make them reflect your *own* understanding and knowledge; highly personal to you.
● Use space in a varied, interesting and more visually recallable way. Each card can be unique, making it very much easier to recall the information.

● You can use colour, boxes and underlining together with graphics, cartoons or diagrams to add vividness to each card. You could use a standardised colour system for your notes: black for information, blue for cross-referencing your own thoughts; green for headings; red for key names, dates, book titles. You can train yourself to recall both *what* you wrote and *where* it was located on the card.

Associating the two will aid your recall of the card.

Some of the other useful aids are included in the outline of a revision card, below. Two completed cards, although reproduced without colour, give some idea of how to construct them.

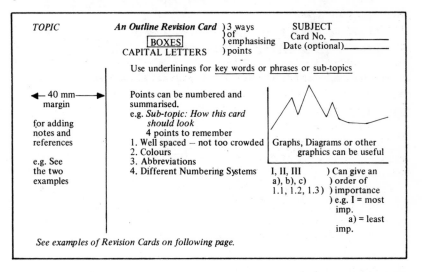

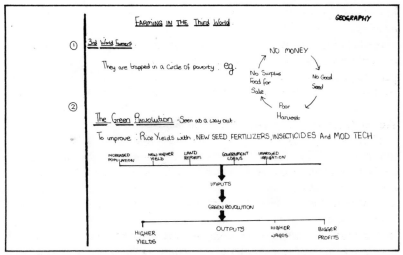

BIOLOGY

②The cropping system.
Crop protectⁿ only 1 feature of farmers strategy.

8 points
Maximize yield          M, D, V, Y, M, P, S, L.
Domesticatⁿ pls
Vigorous selectⁿ
yield hardiness, convenience of harvest
Modificatⁿ of structure ~ soil, fertilizer : Env. fertility
Pure stands
Shortage of sp. nutrients : effect on pest /path. / weeds
Levels of organisatⁿ of cropping system. ✻

1 - 8 all interacting & effecting each other.

**Three basic rules in using abbreviations** are:—
(1)  Be consistent in your use of your own abbreviations. Find a system
     and a set of standard abbreviations and stick to it.
(2)  Do not use abbreviations in work designed to be read by others, e.g.
     examiners. The exceptions to this are relatively few (e.g. i.e, et al,
     viz. are most common).
(3)  Keep a note of your own common abbreviations, either in a note
     book, on a card or at the front of your file.
  In addition, you can devise your own abbreviations for the common
terms used in the subjects you study. These would include:—

— The subjects themselves e.g. G = Geography; M.S. = Materials
  Science.
— The names of professions e.g. Scs = Scientists; Ecs = Economists;
  Hs = Historians.
— Concepts, ideas, principles, common practices e.g. c.w. = casework;
  Cht. = Chartism; strat. = stratification.

You can also abbreviate by:—
— Leaving out unnecessary words thus leaving only the key words you
  need to retain an understanding of what you have written e.g. a, the.
  Shortening the ends of words e.g. —ing becomes g.
— Leaving out syllables e.g. transport becomes t'port.
— Using fore-shortened versions of words you use frequently e.g. cd
  = could; wd = would; shd = should; w/o = without.

## Useful standard abbreviations

Some of the most common and useful abbreviations you can use in note taking and key word revision cards.

| | |
|---|---|
| p | = page |
| pp/ps | = pages |
| f | = following page |
| ff | = following pages |
| ib,ibid | = ibidem = in the same book, chapter, passage, notes |
| e.g. | = exampli gratia = for example |
| op cit | = opere citato = in the work quoted |
| et al | = et alia = and others |
| viz | = videlicet = namely |
| i.e. | = id est = that is |
| cf | = confero = compare |
| c | = circa = about, approximately |
| v/vs | = versus = against |
| inf | = infra = below |
| NB | = nota bene = note well |
| ref | = with reference to |
| esp | = especially |
| = | = equals, is the same as |
| ≠ | = does not equal, is different from |
| < | = less than |
| > | = greater than |
| ∴ | = therefore |
| ∵ | = because |
| no. | = number |
| qv. | = see |
| ∼ | = about |
| → | = it follows |
| alt | = alternative |
| fr | = from |
| exc | = except |
| incl | = including |
| opp | = opposite |
| neg | = negative |
| pos | = positive |
| usu | = usually |

● *The best way of remembering* is to have a real *understanding* of a topic which has been achieved *by finding the right questions to ask and seeking answers to them.* In this way, you come to see the connections between things; how A links with B, B with C and so on.

Such understanding can be developed by some of the ideas that follow, which will aid your recall of information.

## Association

Words, numbers or pictures take meaning in relation to the information around them. It is these *links* with the information around them which fundamentally affects their meaning.

A simple *example* would be the word LOVE. Its meaning and context changes with the words around it. LOVE, Forty; the LOVE bug; I LOVE you; God of LOVE — all conjure up very different perspectives.

Where these links — these associations — form in chains, you may find that a real and lasting understanding develops. Even if this fails to happen, association techniques, both *visual* and *verbal,* can aid your memory very effectively.

## Use your eyes for visual recall

There are three parts to recalling an accurate picture of what you've just seen or read. The first part is to properly attend to it, checking you know how it *looks.* The second is remain *relaxed and calm* whilst *recalling the picture*, which is the third — and equally essential part. It is essential that in this stage you keep your eyes in a position above the horizon i.e. you don't allow your eyes to drop down. For visual eye movements are upward eye movements. Most people picture a familiar scene e.g. the inside of their bedroom, by looking to the centre or to the left of the centre to recall the picture. You may find it helps to gaze into the distance, ignoring your surroundings or to close your eyes. Try it. If you try to recall the same scene with your eyes looking downward, is it as easy?

Exactly the same principle applies to trying to *spell* words accurately, for all good spellers are *visual* recallers. Test somebody who's a good speller and they'll either write it down on paper so they can *see* the word or they'll use an upward eye movement (often to the left of centre or to the centre distance) to read off the letters, or groups of letters of the word they've seen.

## Visual association

Write and draw patterned notes, spider diagrams, key word revision cards and lists. Make them as colourful, well spaced, bold and clear as possible to enable you to visualise them, i.e. recall the exact way they appear.

Create a picture in your imagination to which you link facts. This can be real or imaginary. If you use a real scene you could imagine your room, the kitchen, your street or other familiar places, associating particular facts with particular objects. You can have several different places and associate a topic with each.

You could also use a technique the Romans and Greeks used for remembering. They imagined themselves walking through a palace and pausing at particular doors, stairways or passages associating them with particular facts.

*Grouping items* together and forming links and associations between them in your mind. You could practise this idea by the tray exercise, a well known game played at parties. The object is to remember items on a tray, by associating one with another in practical ways, e.g. scissors cutting string and paper; pens writing on paper; pens kept in a jar. You can find these kinds of associations with objects located next to each other.

## Verbal Association

*Group words* together, e.g. to remember port and starboard and their coloured lights on a boat:
Right — Starboard — Green are the three longer words,
Left — Port — Red are the three shorter words.

*Pair words* — Seek words that match/complement each other or are opposites to each other in order to aid the memory of both.

*Link words and phrases* with those already known to you.

*Unlikely associations* — Look for humorous, bizarre, exotic and colourful associations between facts, ideas and other information. *Opposites* can also be used as an aid to memory.

*Make up a story* — Form several words you want to remember into a story. The words appear in the story in the same sequence as you wish them to appear in answer to question.

## Repetition

Write out things several times. This can help with spelling words, learning tables, learning definitions and dates when events occurred.

Repeat aloud several times. Do this to learn tables, quotations, poems and other extracts from literature.

Listen several times to a record or tape. Read into the tape recorder and replay it to yourself several times. Listen to it as you fall asleep at night.

Re-read information several times. By itself this is not as effective as when coupled with a questioning and/or association technique.

## Mnemonic devices

Mnemonics are devised for artificially aiding the memory. There are several of these, some of which are very familiar.

> *First letter mnemonics*
> Two examples — the colours of a rainbow/spectrum.
> **R**ichard **O**f **Y**ork **G**ave **B**attle **I**n **V**ain
> **R**ed **O**range **Y**ellow **G**reen **B**lue **I**ndigo **V**iolet
>
> Remember the sequence of
> **N**orth **E**ast **S**outh **W**est by linking them with **N**ever **E**at **S**hredded **W**heat

This can be combined with a visual image, moving clockwise around the circle.

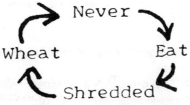

This use of the first letter in a word to construct a more vivid, memorable sentence is used in Several Science subjects, e.g. Biology, as well as in subjects like History and Economics. *Words* can also be made from first letters.

## Rhymes

Familiar uses are for days of the month; 'Thirty days hath September, etc' and in the spelling rule 'i before e except after c'. You can invent your own rhymes or use those which exist already in a particular subject.

## Spelling association

Where there is a confusion between the spelling of similar sounding words with different meanings, the correct spelling can be remembered by associating the spelling with that of an associated object, e.g. stationary and stationery: stationery and envelopes.

## Number rhyme systems

This device is explained in Buzan (1974). A number is associated with an object with which it rhymes, e.g. four/door; five/hive. To remember a piece of information you link it with the number rhyme and create a picture which is as vivid, bizarre or humorous as possible involving the piece of information with the door or hive as the case may be.

## Testing yourself

**A basic revision method** and the use of **key word revision cards** demonstrate the importance of testing yourself in memorising.

Wherever possible, learn topics in a logical whole unit, looking for the natural breaks between topics. Where the whole topic feels too much to revise as one unit, break it down into logical sub-topics or parts.

*Don't learn* all the parts separately and then test yourself. Build up your learning by revising the first part and testing yourself on it before revising the second. Test yourself on the first two parts before moving on to the third part and so on.

*Finally, you are likely to recall most readily:*
— The facts you learn first (Primacy).
— The things you work at most frequently (Frequency).
— The topics you have studied most recently (Recency).
— Topics you worked at with maximum concentration and intensity.

## Revising Problem Solving (mathematically based) Science and Technology Subjects

**Repetition** and **mnemonics** can both be used to learn formulae, tables, sequences etc. Other memorising ideas will suit particular topics or questions. Some particularly useful approaches are:—

● To practise answering questions, both in *full* and in *outline.* Do this as often as possible. From an early stage, reduce the amount of time you allow yourself so that by the time you are close to the examinations you are allowing yourself no more time than you would have in the exam room.

● Practise diagrams and any other visual material without looking at the original book or notes. Upon completing them, compare them with the original, repeating the process until you can draw an adequate representation of the original without errors.

● Use key word revision cards to practise recall of formulae, symbols, etc. and for keeping your diagram outlines.

# How To . . . Books
# Opening Doors of Opportunity

A major series of self-help paperbacks packed with valuable information on new opportunities in today's fast-changing world. Each of these user-friendly handbooks gives clear up-to-date information and advice, prepared by experts, and complete with checklists for action and self-assessment material. The guides will save you time and money by supplying essential information which is often hard to find.

Helpfully clear layout with illustrations and cartoons, glossary, useful sources, index. Each 215 x 135mm, £4.95 approx.

You can't afford to miss the 'How To . . . series'

**How to Get That Job** Joan Fletcher
A guide for job hunters of all ages.
0 7463 0326 2

**How to Raise Business Finance** Peter Ibbetson
A down-to-earth guide for the self-employed and small business needing financial assistance.
0 7463 0338 6

**How to Live and Work in Australia** Laura Veltman
The unique handbook for all those considering employment and residence 'Down Under'.
0 7463 0331 9

**How to Live and Work in America** Steve Mills
Packed with new ideas on home life, leisure, travel, social and business opportunities.
0 7463 0323 8

**How to Help Your Child at School** John West-Burnham
Vital information and advice for every concerned parent.
0 7463 0329 7

**How to Enjoy Retirement** Harry Gray
Utilising a lifetime's skills and experience for a happy and productive retirement.
0 7463 0323 8

**How to Claim State Benefits** Martin Rathfelder
Making sense of the system.
0 7463 0505 2

Dozens more titles in preparation. For details please contact Dept BPA.

Northcote House Publishers Ltd., Harper & Row House,
Estover Road, Plymouth PL6 7PZ, United Kingdom.
Tel: Plymouth (0752) 705251 Telex: 45635.

# 3
# Taking Exams

Problem checklist
Know your examinations
Recording exam information
Contingency plans
Getting used to exams
Knowing what examiners want
I'm worried that . . .
Using the last few hours
Techniques in the exam room
At the start of your exam
Underlining key words
Types of questions
Writing a model essay
Multiple-choice questions
Common problems
The aftermath

| I have/may have problems with:— | Tick √ if it applies to you | Brief Tips | Where to find out more (pp.) |
|---|---|---|---|
| knowing enough about what I have to do in the exams | | Check you know the number of papers, questions and instructions to candidates. Are there any changes this year? Speak to your teachers/lecturers | 51-52 |
| getting started in the exam | | Read instructions carefully. Read carefully through all the exam paper. Underline important words. Make brief answer plans. | 60-63 66 |
| knowing which question to answer first | | Most students answer their best question first. Examiners agree that this is a good idea. | 66 |
| never having taken such an important exam before | | You don't have to be brilliant to pass exams. Be positive. Know the standard expected of you beforehand. | 54-57 |
| settling down in the exam room | | Be methodical. Read instructions: have pens etc. ready. Read all questions. Learn some relaxation techniques in case they are needed. | 60, 84, 94, 101-103 |
| getting used to taking exams | | Practise answering old exam questions in exam conditions with the same amount of time as in the exam. | 54-55 |
| knowing what examiners are looking for | | Examiners are looking to give marks, not to take them away. They are looking for answers that actually answer the question. | 55-56 |
| knowing how much time to give to each question in the exam | | Take away at least 30 mins. of a 3 hour exam for reading instructions, choosing questions, planning answers etc. Divide the rest of the time equally. | 59-63 |
| fearing I will not be able to answer any questions when I read through the exam paper | | This is often caused by reading through the paper too quickly. Read it again, underlining all important words in each question. Learn to think more positively. | 61-63 84-85 103 |
| making sure I read each question properly | | Underline words in questions. Try writing brief outline notes (linear or patterned) as a first answer to the question | 62-65 |
| wondering if I know enough to pass | | Use the symbols described in *What should I revise?* Concentrate on what you are doing, not on worrying. | 21-26 79-83 |
| wondering if I will be penalised for my spelling, handwriting or use of grammar | | It is important to be legible with the minimum of grammar and spelling errors but examiners are often instructed not to penalise this unduly in exams. | 69-70 |
| not being able to write fast enough; running out of time | | Write in shorter sentences if you struggle to express yourself. Most people run out of time: timed questions will minimise the effect of doing so. Exercise your fingers — *A Do-it-Yourself Guide to Muscular Relaxation.* | 69, 101 |
| not answering all questions in full | | If time is running out, answer two half-questions. This can gain more marks than one longer answer and a missed question. | 59-63 69 |
| planning outline answers in the exam room | | Practise this technique in revision as part of testing yourself. You do not have to write these outlines but they often help. | 27-28 39-40 62-63 |
| | | | |

One way of checking that you know what each examination requires of you is to answer the following questions, where they apply to a subject.

(1)  How many papers do you have to sit?

(2)  What time is allowed for each paper?

(3)  How many questions do you have to answer? How many questions are there to choose from?

(4)  Do you have to answer questions from particular sections?

(5)  Are there any compulsory questions?

(6)  Are all questions worth equal marks? If not, which questions are worth more?

(7)  What is the maximum time you could allow yourself for each question in order to divide your time equally?

(8)  How are marks proportioned between coursework (C), laboratory (L) or workshop (W), project work (P) and examinations (E)?

(9)  Are marks linked between one year's examinations and another? (This occurs more frequently in some further and higher education exams).

(10) How long, at maximum, could you allow yourself for preparation in the exam, e.g. jotting down some outline answers?

If you don't know the answers to these questions, check with teachers and past papers, ensuring no changes have occurred since the last time candidates sat the examination.

You can use this table to write down your answers to the ten questions for each examinable subject. Sub-divide subjects where there is more than one paper.

Two examples are given as guidelines.

| How to express your answer | As a number | In hours and minutes | No. Questions to answer No. Questions to choose from | Sections and Numbers | (If Applicable) Section and Q. No. | Note differences in marks, if any, where known | In minutes | In percentages | Yes/No Years/ | Minutes |
|---|---|---|---|---|---|---|---|---|---|---|
| Subjects: two Examples | Q1 | Q2 | Q3 | Q4 | Q5 | Q6 | Q7 | Q8 | Q9 | Q10 |
| Mathematics | 1 | 2½ hr. | 10/14 | Sect A-4 Sect B-3 Sect C-3 | No | Equal | 12-15 mins. | E 100% | No | 20-30 mins. |
| Geography | 1 | 3 hrs. | 5/9 | Sect A-1 Sect B-2 Sect C-2 | Q1 Sect A | Q1 = 40% Others = 15% ea. | Q1 - 50-60 mins. Others = 20-25 mins. | P = 20% E = 80% | Yr 1 = 30% Yr 2 = 70% | 30-40 mins. |
| *Your Exam Subjects* | | | | | | | | | | |
| | | | | | | | | | | |
| | | | | | | | | | | |
| | | | | | | | | | | |
| | | | | | | | | | | |
| | | | | | | | | | | |
| | | | | | | | | | | |
| | | | | | | | | | | |

It will benefit you to make plans before the exams begin, particularly if you anticipate difficulties.

## Health

*Health issues* are one obvious example. Hay fever, for example, is quite a common complaint in summer examinations, particularly when the pollen count is high. Ensuring an adquate supply of medicines, nose spray, etc. can minimise its effect. Period pains would be another example where medical help beforehand, e.g. pain killers, may reduce problems.

It may be appropriate as well to inform your examination centre i.e. normally your school or college, if your symptoms are apt to be severe. They are able to inform the Examining Boards of any information you pass on. Your papers will be marked in the usual way and then any information from the Centre will be considered. Exactly the same principle applies to illness that occurs in the examination room.

Tell someone if you're not well.

## Spare pens and equipment

*Spare pens* and equipment are another example of preparing yourself appropriately in advance.

## Arriving late

You would normally be allowed, by most examination regulations, to enter an exam room up to half-an-hour late, if you find yourself delayed. *If you do arrive late,* do not allow yourself to be panicked. Stick to a revised and foreshortened time budget with the aim of attempting *all* the questions you have been asked to complete.

## The place and time

Finding out exactly *where the exam is held*, how long it takes to reach the place, and exactly what time the examination begins and ends will enable you to plan in advance. For example, you will be able to note actual times for reading the paper, answering the first question, beginning the second and subsequent questions.

## Coping with anxiety

Learning and practising the *relaxation, positive thinking and panic coping* techniques in the **Coping with Anxiety** section will also prepare you for all eventualities in the examination room.

Although some people appear to take examinations in their stride, for the rest of us the feelings associated with examinations make it very difficult to get used to them. However, if we can familiarise ourselves with what is expected of us beforehand, it may well help to lessen their impact upon us and enable us to cope better in the examination room.

### Know what the examination examines

Use the guidelines in **Know your examination** and **Recording Exam information** to get a clear picture of the structure of the examination.

Add to this conversations with teachers/lecturers for their guidelines; looking at the syllabus (when it is available); surveying all your notes and other work from the course; reviewing past exam papers and making use of the ideas in **Devise questions around a topic** (see p.26).

### Practise answering questions in examination conditions

Simulate examination conditions by answering a question *in silence without* the aid of *books or other materials; at a desk* and within strictly applied *examination time limit*.

You can do this for:—
- individual questions
- a whole paper (2, 2½ or 3 hours)
- planning outline answers (linear, spider or patterned notes).

This will provide practice at thinking clearly and quickly in examination conditions. You may wish to try these approaches gradually e.g. giving yourself less time each time to answer the question; working for a longer silent period each time.

You could add to this:—
- Using a friend or parent as an invigilator, so you can get used to someone walking past you or standing behind you.
- Sitting in the room where you will sit the exam to get the feel of it.

### Learn from Mock Exams or Tests

Once you have completed your mock exams, engage in a full post-mortem of them by yourself or with the help of another. Whether they went well or badly, use the **Problem Checklists** to analyse what happened. Check your revision, exam techniques and your anxiety levels. *Write down* the changes you will make and start to put them into operation immediately.

### Know the standard expected of you

You don't have to be brilliant to pass examinations or to do very well in them.

*Two guidelines* to standards expected come from:—
- Comments as well as marks on your work during the course.
- Any examples of model answers by lecturers, teachers or Examination Boards. These may also come from good answers to questions by other students known to you.

*Two guidelines* to standards that students have used are:—
- The average student who completes an average amount of course work, expends an average amount of effort and develops an average understanding should pass the exam.
- By revising half the syllabus, the candidate will be able to answer around half the questions in the exam and with half marks gained on each will pass.

Neither of *these two guidelines* are exactly accurate. They could, in fact, be *misleading*. If the 'average' students in your group have not yet achieved a pass standard in their work, the first guideline is unlikely to be true. It is possible to revise half the syllabus but omit to revise some of the most important, and frequently occurring, topics in which case the second guideline is unlikely to be true. There are, too, other exceptions, e.g. certain medical or Taxation professional examinations where a high degree of technical knowledge and understanding is demanded.

However, the *spirit* of these two statements is very useful. It is that *the vast majority of examinations are not as difficult as students believe them to be*.

## Know what examiners want — and don't want

| Examiners DO want | Examiners DO NOT want |
|---|---|
| To give marks. Examiners are often teachers and lecturers sympathetic to students. In many internal exams they will be your *own* lecturers and teachers, with good reasons to seek to award you marks. | To take marks away. (Examiners are not poised with red pens ready to penalise your mistakes). |
| You to answer the question that has been set. | Waffle and bluffing which may irritate them: to be told all the candidate knows about a topic, whether it answers the question or not. |
| Scripts to be legible. They have a large number to read in a short time with same fee for each script. | Illegibility. See *Legibillity* (p.69) |
| All the required number of questions to be attempted | Extra questions to be attempted. Not only do they not gain more marks, but the reverse is usually true as answers tend to be shorter. Fewer than the required number of questions to be attempted. They are disappointed for the candidate. |
| Short, simple sentences and a direct style of writing. | Over-elaborateness, over-wordiness. |
| Opinions to be backed by relevant argument. | Unsubstantiated opinion, i.e. 'I think' or 'I believe' without adequate explanation or argument for the belief. In Social Science, the use of 'I . . .' in this manner is frequently frowned upon and opinions are expressed impersonally. |
| All parts of a question to be answered. | You to neglect the second part of a question, which is frequently worth the same marks as the first part. (A common fault of candidates). |
| Appropriate examples and illustrations. | A catalogue of examples before a point is properly explained. |
| Standard English | The use of slang or spoken expressions, particularly at the beginning of sentences e.g. 'Yes, you can please some of the people . . .'; 'Well . . .'; 'As I was saying. . . .'. |
| You to answer the question immediately you start to write. | You to copy out the question, unless you are specifically asked to do so. Long background introductions to the topic. |
| Humour — intentional or unintentional*!* | To be bored by a candidate who has evidently put little effort into the exam. |

\* Other guidelines are included in *Writing Essay-type answers*

## Dispel irrational beliefs about exams

Three common beliefs what are held about exams and their outcomes are:—

● My future will be ruined if I fail/fail to get the grades I want.
● I'm just no good at exams. Some people are; I'm not.
● Exams get more difficult as you work through the educational system

Each of these has elements of irrational, or falsely held beliefs in it.

**My future will be ruined if I fail/fail to get the grades I want**

Examinations are an important way in which professional groups in our society select for their membership. Success in them does open doors to particular jobs and careers. Lack of success will mean certain jobs and careers are not immediately open to you, at least at the level of entry you originally intended. Some may be closed altogether.

However, happiness, wealth, peace of mind, rich experience of life, meaningful status in the eyes of others, a worthwhile career, a useful job and an inner sense of purpose and self belief as a human being, do not depend upon examination results. The world is teeming with people who have found that to be the case whether they passed examinations or not.

**I'm just no good at exams. Some people are; I'm not**

There are two elements in this view. One is that your past performance will determine any future attempts. The other is in comparing yourself to others you find your performance inadequate. The answer to the first element is that the past frequently *is* escapable. By buying this book and reading this page, you have set out to become 'good at exams'. Other people are largely irrelevant. They do not depend for their success upon your lack of success or vice versa.

**Exams get more difficult as you work your way through the educational system**

Difficulty is a relative world. What is difficult at one age is not at another; what is difficult when you are inexperienced in an activity is not when you are experienced; what is difficult to one person is not to another; what is difficult on one day is not on another.

Certainly, examinations demand more specialist knowledge, understanding and expertise, as you move through their different levels. They may become more technical, involve more abstract ideas and concepts, involve you in greater specialisation and more specialist jargon. This does not mean they become more difficult.

In some ways, you could argue that the first external-type examinations you take are the most difficult (GCSE or 'O' levels) because they are unfamiliar. You have had little or no opportunity to develop an expertise in taking them. With more experience and appropriate techniques, they can become easier for many students.

Finally, I believe the difficulty of all examinations is exaggerated by many students. Exams are easier than is often believed.

**On the night before the examination**

● Review your key word cards with the emphasis on practising recall. Attempting to cram in *new* material, although tempting, will tend to use up energy and be self-defeating.

● Check you have all the equipment — pens, pencils, instruments, etc. — you need and are allowed to take into the exam room. Several different shaped pens may ease the pressure points on your fingers and thumbs.

● Check your timetable as to the right time and place of the exam. Make sure you have any candidate's number or any other administrative items you need.

● Check your personal timetable for the next morning, checking the times you need to get up, gather your materials, leave the house, etc.

● Use any of the ideas you have developed from the **Coping with Anxiety** section to aid your relaxation and to sleep.

**On the day of the examination**

● Try as far as possible to stick to your normal routine.

● If you do normally eat breakfast, take it as normal for you will be using up a considerable amount of energy. If you don't eat breakfast normally, consider eating something light. If this does not seem possible, you could consider taking some glucose tablest, barley sugar or mints with you for the examination room: for most external examinations unobtrusive sweet sucking would be permitted.

● Don't drink too much in the morning. Part of the normal reaction to exams is a state of appropriate nervous tension and arousal you may feel. This may well cause more visits to the lavatory then usual, which is a perfectly normal — and appropriate — reaction. You don't, however, want the need to continue in the exam room, if it can be avoided!

● Check your personal timetable made the night before to ensure all is going to time, occupying spare time you have constructively by doing something positive or relaxing.

● Check you have all your equipment before you leave home.

● You can take *brief* looks at your revision card summaries, re-checking your recall.

● Use the deep breathing and other relaxation techniques when you feel the need for them. You may also find the ideas in **On the Way to the Exam** and **The Morning before an afternoon exam** helpful (see p.88).

**A summary**

This outline is adapted from one used by Rowntree (1976), in his useful book 'Learn how to study'.

---

*Settle and compose yourself*

*Read right through the paper* (5 minutes)
Check instructions.
Underline key words in questions — add one or two lines.
Choose your best questions, using a symbol system.

*Plan your time*
Divide according to marks per question.
Write down finishing time for each question.
If possible, plan in 10 mintes, checking time at end.

*Plan your answers*
Brief notes on main ideas and important details.
Linear, spider or pattern note outline.
Outline all answers at beginning (if doubtful of remembering);
or one at a time or a few answers together.
Leave space after each question.

*Priorities*
Answer your best question first.
Stick to the time allowed for each question: marks for two half questions are worth more than one.
Stick to what the questions are asking.

*Write*
Simply, in short sentences, checking spellings.
Legibly.

*At the end of the exam:*
If there is time left, check your answers.
Minimise your conversations.

---

### Getting settled

*Settle and compose yourself.* Set out any pens, pencils, rulers, rubbers and other permitted equipment. Check your watch with the clock in the room, which should be visible to you. If it is not visible to you, place your watch where you can easily see it. This is the moment to practice all the ideas for positive alert performance described in the **Coping with Anxiety** section e.g. **Visualising the Examination.**

### Read right through the paper

Read right through the exam paper. *Allow yourself at least five minutes for this. In particular, re-check that the Instructions are as you expected as in* **Know your Examinations, Recording Exam information.** *Note* the length of the exam and write down the finishing time; any compulsory questions; the number of questions to be answered in total and from which sections of the paper they are to be selected.

● If you tend to be anxious about finding your hoped-for questions appearing in the examination paper, read through the paper *not expecting* the questions you want to appear. *Expect it* to be difficult to find enough questions to answer. Adopting this approach you will probably find your hopes raised rather than dashed and it will help you look at each question much more carefully. This is not designed to be the opposite of a positive approach, simply a steadying, realistic approach.

Pay particular attention to what the question is asking. It is very easy to jump to incorrect conclusions about the meaning of a question. A common explanation for this is anxiety to find certain topics or questions causes *a word or phrase* to be selected from a question and assumed to be the topic or particular question. We want to find certain questions so we *do* them, whether or not they are really worded as we wish them to be! In the same way, other questions, which may well be more appropriate questions to choose, are dismissed because a key word or phrase does not appear when it is said quickly for the first time.

One way to prevent this happening is to develop the technique of **Underlining Key Words in questions.**

One outcome of underlining can be to discover that simply worded questions are not always the easiest to attempt. Questions which require careful reading can be easier for you to answer once you have clearly understood them.

### Plan your time

● You can plan the outline of the time you will allocate in an exam, before the day of the examination. If you **Know your Examinations** and know the start and finishing times you can make a rough plan of your time allocation. During the examination itself, write down the planned finishing time for each question. Divide the time according to marks allocated per question and marks allocated per part of a question. (Increasingly, Examination Boards are including this information.)

● Stick to your time budget. As explained in **If you are running out of time**, two half answered questions will usually obtain more marks than one completed question and one unanswered question.

● Use any time remaining at the end of the exam to check your answers for 10 minutes. Many students never have this checking time at the end and it is by no means essential that you plan it in.

## Plan your answers

You can use brief notes to outline an answer to the question. You may decide that you would prefer to get straight on with your answer. As long as you have a clear idea of what you wish to write in your answers there is no problem with this approach. You should do what suits you best.

● You can find examples of outline notes in **Using underlined words to form an outline answer** and in *Spider diagrams* and *Pattern Notes* (see p.27).

● If you are using this type of outline plan, it can be a useful approach to outline all your answers in one working spell at the beginning of the exam. Alternatively, you can plan one answer at a time or two or three together before commencing to write out your full answers. The advantage of planning all your answers at the beginning is that it enables you to record a considerable amount of information whilst it is fresh in your mind; it removes the anxiety that you will forget it by the time you come to answer a later question. It also gives you notes to fall back on if you run out of time. In an emergency, you could refer the examiner to them, if they are readable and comprehensible. You can also add to these notes during the course of the exam when you think of other points you have remembered: answering one question often throws up associations with another topic or question.

● Leaving spaces after each answer will enable you to add to it, if you recall more information.

● Do not allow yourself to get stuck on a stubborn problem. Return to it later. A change of question can often enable you to gain a fresh perspective on the previous question.

## Underlining key words in questions

Answering an exam question correctly depends upon understanding it clearly in the first place.

A useful technique is to *underline*, after careful consideration, the most *important words, phrases* or *data* in the question.

Although you often end up underlining most of the words in a question, it is *where the lines are drawn* and where the *spaces between lines occur* which draws your attention to the exact meaning of the question.

If the words which tell you the *type* of question are *underlined twice* (or in a different colour), it will ensure you take the right approach with your answer.

In conclusion, this technique has several advantages:

- It ensures you read the question properly and note *exactly* what it is asking. It is very easy, in your anxiety to find a question you can answer and to get started, to misread a question. This can cause you to ignore a question which it would be quite possible for you to answer and to choose to answer a question which turns out to be different from your original perception of it.

- It draws your attention to the *approach* that examiners want you to take, i.e. the type of question it is.

- It provides you with the key words to start a *brief outline answer* plan.

## Some examples

Q.1 <u>Give an account</u> of the <u>digestion</u>, <u>absorption</u> and <u>use</u> of <u>carbohydrates.</u>

Q.2 <u>Describe why beef farms</u> are the <u>main</u> type of <u>agriculture</u> in the <u>central lowlands</u> of <u>Scotland.</u>

Q.3 <u>What is meant</u> by an <u>acid</u> and a <u>molar solution</u> of an <u>acid?</u>

- In order to test whether you have underlined the correct words to enable you to fully and exactly understand the question *say the words you have underlined quietly aloud to yourself.*
- Practise this underlining technique with questions from past papers or questions you are currently answering.

## Using underlined words to form an outline answer

You can use the underlined words to form an outline answer, either in linear or pattern/spider form.

## A patterned or spider outline

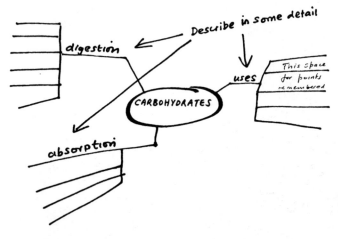

## A Linear outline

Carbohydrates Give account = *describe in some detail*

1 *Digestion* — points remembered

                —

2 *Absorption* —

                —

3 *Use* —

                —

# Types of questions

Questions in examinations vary in the approach they ask you to take. In every question there are certain key words (a number of these are verbs) which tell you the type of question it is and exactly which approach the examiner wishes you to take.

Two common groupings are *descriptive* and *analytical* questions. Below are listed fifteen descriptive and nineteen analytical words and phrases which occur commonly. Each is then defined.

## Descriptive

*Define* — set down the precise meaning of a word or phrase. Show that the distinctions implied in the definition are necessary.

*Describe* — give a detailed or graphic account of.

*Distinguish between* — note the difference between.

*Give an account of* — describe in some detail.

*How* . . . — in what way, by what means or method, to what extent.

*Illustrate* — use a figure or diagram to explain or clarify, *or* make it clear by the use of concrete examples.

*Outline* — describe without detail, summarise.

*Relate* — narrate (the more usual meaning in examinations): to show how things are connected and to what extent they are alike or affect each other.

*State* — present in brief, clear form.

*Show how* — make clear by what means.

*Summarise* — give a concise account of the chief points or substance of a matter, omitting details and examples.

*Trace* — follow the development or history of a topic from some point of origin.

*What* . . . — of which kind, which?

*When* . . . — at what time, on which day or year, etc.?

*Where* . . . — at/to what place, in what particular?

## Analytical

*Account for* — explain.

*Analyse* — make a detailed description and criticism of.

*Argue the case for* — back your opinion by reasoning in favour of it.

*Assess* — determine the amount or value of.

*Calculate* — reckon or compute by mathematics.

*Comment upon* — offer an opinion (avoiding the use of 'I. . .').

*Compare* — look for similarities and differences between.

*Consider* — express your thoughts and observations about.

*Contrast* — set in opposition in order to bring out differences.

*Criticise* — give your judgment about the merit of theories or opinions or about the truth of facts, and back by a discussion of the evidence.

*Discuss* — investigate or examine by argument, giving reasons pro and con.

*Evaluate* — make an appraisal of the worth of something, in the light of its truth or utility.

*Examine )* — inquire into, attempt to discover, investigate,

*Explore )* approach in a questioning manner.

*Explain* — make plain, interpret, account for, illustrate the meaning of.

*Interpret* — expound the meaning of; make clear and explicit; usually giving your own judgment also.

*Justify* — show adequate grounds for decisions or conclusions.

*Review* — to make a survey of, examining the subject critically.

*Why. . .* — for what reason(s).

## Other types of questions

*Some questions combine both types of question* as the examiner looks for a combination of facts and analysis, as in 'Describe and explain'.

*Quotations* usually indicate some kind of *analysis* is required.

*'Brief'* or *'List'* mean what they say. A paragraph for the first and a straightforward descriptive list, such as that above.

*'Compare and Contrast'* type questions require you to point out the similarities and differences between two items, events or ideas. A good answer would focus on one *aspect* at a time and find the differences and similarities.

*An example* — Q.Compare and Contrast cars and motor-bikes.

The same applies to *'For and Against'* type questions, where, although you can argue all the points 'for' and then all the points, 'against' separately the answers which effectively argue for and against aspect-by-aspect can be the most successful.

In social science subjects such as History, Sociology and Economics, it is important to distinguish whether the examiner is asking you about the *causes* or *reasons for* or whether you are being asked about the *results of* events or actions.

● 'Factors', 'Account for', 'What problems faced?' — suggest you should write about reasons and causes.

● Achievements', 'Effects', 'Impact', 'How successful', 'The importance of' — suggest you should write about the results or consequences of an event, an idea or action.

## Choosing the questions you will answer

Use some simple symbol systems to indicate your reaction to each question, once you have carefully read it and decided exactly what it is asking. Guidelines that can be used are:—

- Use a simple star system (up to 3 or 5 stars ***) next to each question: Choose the questions with the highest star rating.
- Use the EASY/DIFFICULT and KNOW/UNDERSTAND symbols from **Deciding what to revise?** choosing those questions on the positive end of scale.
- Give the questions scores out of 10 to indicate your confidence in answering them.
- Number the questions in the order you will answer them, choosing your best question first; then second best, third best and so on.

## Writing essay-type answers

You cannot exactly reproduce in the exam room an essay you wrote on the same question as part of your course-work. The time constraints in an exam are different and a more direct precise style is more appropriate for most examinations.

Here are some of the principal guidelines.

- Try to lay out your answer so that it looks attractive, particularly where your comprehension of the English language is being tested.
- Do not waste time copying out the question (unless asked).
- Write in continuous prose, not notes.
- Decide whether it is a descriptive or analytical essay you are being asked to write. Use **Underlining key words** and **Types of questions** to help you decide.
- Keep your essay plan close by so that you can refer to it with ease.
- Avoid repetition, vagueness, generalisations and waffle.
- Use short paragraphs as well as simple, shorter sentences.

Exam essays have a beginning, a middle and an end. The beginning *Introduction* will have several of these features:

- a summary of what you are about to argue or describe.
- an indication of your attitude to the question asked.
- the key words from the question incorporated into the above, to indicate that you have read and understood the question.
- a back-up reason for any first statements made. This can be expanded upon or added to in the middle.
- definitions of any terms that clearly need to be defined in order for you to proceed with your answer.
- it will be one or two paragraphs long.
- it will indicate that more needs to be described, explained or argued to clarify what has been said so far.

It is my experience that introductions to essays are often of a very poor standard. Some candidates obviously get stuck in trying to express themselves. You can feel they are wondering what to write. Others simply restate the title and say something like "I will now go on to answer the question": a poor start. Yet others start a long, long background account of a situation, event, period, etc. before beginning to make any relevant points in answer to the question. So I would suggest if you find introductions to essays difficult you try some of these alternatives:

- Practise them before the exam, using the principles outlined.
- Write a very short, one or two sentence, introduction before moving on to the essential core of the essay — the middle part.
- Don't waste time thinking of 'special' things to say in an introduction. Get on with answering the question in a straightforward manner, using your plan.

## The middle

The middle will normally contain your *key facts*. They will be expressed *precisely* and *specifically* and in as much *detail* as the question appears to demand. Try to *avoid generalisations* or covering up phrases which attempt to conceal that you can't remember a piece of information.

Assemble your *major facts* in a clear manner and *show* how they are *relevant* to the answer. Where the essay involves you arguing a case, citing reasons, explaining causes, analysing consequences and other forms of *analysis,* let the facts support your arguments.

## The end — your conclusion

Concluding paragraphs are often as inadequate as introductions! As with introductions it is best not to think of them as being special concluding paragraphs.

Ideally, you will reach a coherent logical conclusion at the end of your essay. It does not have to side with any particular issue that the question focusses on. You can argue that the evidence is conflicting, the fors and againsts evenly balanced or that evidence is insufficient. Practise this type of conclusion in your preparation for the examination.

If you find concluding paragraphs difficult, don't over-concern yourself with them. Simply answer the question to the best of your ability and when you have done so — stop.

Finally, in conclusion, try not to start your final paragraphs with 'Finally . . .' or 'In conclusion . . .' It is boring, repetitive and tends to cause examiners to yawn!

*It is important to remember* that the bulk of marks in the vast majority of essay type questions are awarded to the quality of the information and argument that forms the middle of most answers.

## Answering multiple-choice questions and objective tests

The use of multiple-choice examinations is on the increase, although essay-type examinations remain the most common.

Multiple-choice questions, as their name implies, give you a choice of answers to a specific question. By marking a box, in the way you are instructed, you indicate which answer best fits the question. In this way, the multiple-choice exam aims to reward a good grasp of the whole syllabus without placing an undue emphasis upon the candidate's ability to write descriptive answers.

The main points to bear in mind in answering this type of question are:—

- Read the instructions particularly carefully, the time you are allowed and how to complete the answers. As many of these tests and exams are marked by computer it is important that you actually complete your answers in exactly the form required.

- Work straight through the paper, noting the more difficult questions which you can return to later. Once you are sure you have the right answer, don't spend time re-considering.

- Underline key words in the questions to ensure you have read them properly. Particularly be on the lookout for *not* and double negatives in objective tests.

- Pick the alternative that appears to be nearest to the truth. Multiple-choice tests are not purely tests of factual recall. They also test your comprehension and interpretation of information. One statement is going to be closest to the truth. By eliminating the answers you know to be wrong you will limit your choice and improve your chance of answering correctly.

- Don't guess randomly, but make informed guesses when you do not know. However, you should check the marking system, whenever possible, to see if incorrect answers are penalised. If penalties apply, as they do in a number of objective tests, but less often in multiple-choice papers, then be wary of guessing. Leave the difficult questions until later and return to them after completing the section. Reflecting on the question may give you some insight into the answer.

- Multiple-choice papers are not speed tests as such, but do require you to work at a business-like speed. Don't spend a long time puzzling over one or two questions. Continue on through the paper as questions you find easier may well occur throughout the paper. With other objective tests, timed sections do require that you work quickly. Keep your watch in view to time yourself carefully.

## If you are running out of time

Divide whatever time that remains between questions. Examiners share a wide measure of agreement that it is easier to gain five marks in the last questions than an extra five in the question you were last working on. For this reason, two half answered questions usually gain more marks than one more completely answered question with which you have persevered.

With 10 minutes left and one answer to complete, you may revert to an emergency technique. Use brief notes to answer a descriptive (word based) question. Minimise the amount of calculation shown in mathematically-based problem solving subjects (N.B. This latter guideline may not apply equally to students in higher education, where showing all understanding of the *means* of calculation may be an important source of marks.)

Provided these brief outlines are readable and comprehensible to the examiner, they can gain marks. In *most* examinations, Examining Boards lay down criteria for marking brief notes, on a reduced scale of marks.

Alternatively, if you have written readable notes of skeleton outlines at the beginning of the examination, you can refer the examiner to them as your time elapses. If you do this, cross out the work you do not wish the examiner to read (a good principle at the end of an examination).

## Legibility

It is a help to examiners if your handwriting is clear and readable. They will not deliberately penalise illegible handwriting, but examiners are human beings and they are going to be irritated if, because of difficulty in reading your handwriting, it takes them two or three times as long to read your script as it does to read another candidate's script of similar length, content and quality.

As with *spelling* and *grammar,* most Examining Bodies give guidelines to examiners as to how they should treat such scripts and, where penalities are imposed, they will tend to be only a small proportion of the total marks awarded in many examinations, e.g. 5-10%.

However, even if your handwriting is not particularly legible, you could considerably improve its legibility by:

— spacing it out more
— making sure you have no two letters that look exactly alike
— avoiding loops which overlap above and below the line.

*Writing style is not a key factor in most examinations,* unless it is a subject where you are examining literature or grammatical style, e.g. English Literature and Language.

You may wish to impress the examiner with the fluency of your writing and will probably do so, if you succeed. However, it is not desirable to sacrifice facts and arguments for style. Whenever you find yourself with difficulties in expressing yourself, *write in short, direct, simple sentences.* This is a useful guideline for most examination answers.

## After the exam

The problem with analysing what you write with friends or others is that, in my experience, nearly everybody is equally convinced they have missed out key facts, answered questions in the wrong way, miscalculated etc. As a result such post-mortem discussions invariably reduce confidence and serve little purpose. In addition, your memory of what you wrote and its standard is likely to be *imperfect,* even if your recall is *good.* The difference between *what you remember* you wrote and *exactly* what you wrote can make a significant difference to the marks you obtain.

In some circumstances it can be useful to discuss certain issues. For example, where a subject is examined by two separate papers, the topics and types of question which appear in the first can give you guidelines to the topics and questions which may appear in the second paper.

# 4

# Coping with Anxiety

This section of the book contains:—

- Over 30 ideas and practical approaches to coping with anxiety, selected for their relevance to taking examinations. (They will also be relevant to many other situations.) These are selected from a vast range of helpful approaches: more are included in **Further Reading and Help.**

- **An Emergency Quick Relaxation Technique** and other ideas to prevent or cope with panic and overwhelming anxiety.

- Ideas that can be easily understood and many that can quickly be put into practice. Practise them over time to prepare you for the exam.

- Ideas that are designed to help you form the more positive attitudes towards taking examinations and your own capacity to perform well in them.

- Ideas of direct use in refreshing you and in helping you study efficiently and effectively, even if you are coping well with your own anxiety.

| I have/may have problems with | Tick √ if it applies to you | Brief Tips | Where to find out more (pp.) |
|---|---|---|---|
| How anxious to be before an exam | | Some tension and nervous energy can be useful to trigger you to action. | 72 |
| How to cope with panic before or during the exam | | Learn *An Emergency Quick Relaxation Technique, Create a Scene in Your Imagination* and *Breathing Slowly and Deeply.* | 94-95 103 |
| Being unable to concentrate | | See *Improving concentration.* Practise focussing your attention during revision, cutting out distracting sounds. | 32, 104 |
| Getting to sleep at night | | Exercise, warm baths, relaxation exercises and a good sleeping posture can all be useful. | 89-93 |
| How to relax in the exam room | | Learn techniques of muscle tensing and relaxing as well as how to breathe to relax. | 94-104 |
| Whether to take some time off for relaxing and entertainment | | Definitely. Incorporating time off into your revision programme is a part of your revision time not a subtraction from it. | 32-37 73-74 |
| Not being bothered about the exams: anxious because there is no feeling of anxiety at all | | As long as you feel you are working effectively, there is no problem. If you are not, learning some effective revision and anxiety coping techniques may free you to feel anxiety — and cope with it. | 21-47 72-104 |
| How to stop worrying about the amount of work to be done, what others will say | | See *Ways of Coping with Anxiety* and *A Self guidance Checklist to reduce stress* for a large number of ideas to help you. | 73-74 79-81 |

## Introduction

A degree of positive anticipation, in which you are keyed up and ready to work, is appropriate and useful when revising and taking examinations. It can enable you to be more alert, attentive and to concentrate more fully. It can sharpen your exam performance; make you feel more full of energy; cause you to work at the most effective speed and be more attentive to detail.

It is possible to mistake this state of arousal for anxiety. It is also possible for anxiety to become disabling, i.e. to stop you working effectively or at all. Equipped with the practice of these ideas, *you will be able to cope with your anxiety,* no matter how severe or overwhelming it feels using brain arousal to bring you to peak performance.

The approaches are aimed at how you think, feel and behave. As well as suggestions for how to tackle any problems you may have, the approaches are grouped under four headings

Thinking and Anxiety
Breathing Techniques
Muscular Relaxation
Visualisation

The muscular and breathing techniques are natural techniques that work on the central nervous system and auxiliary nervous system: the thinking and visualisation techniques give you self-help approaches to extend the control you are able to exercise over yourself.

**Ways of coping with anxiety**

One or more of the following suggestions may both help you reduce anxiety and work effectively:—

- Adopt positive attitudes, making positive statements to yourself.
- Stop thoughts that worry you.
- Know and adapt to situations that cause you both the most and the least anxiety.
- Rehearse and simulate situations you find difficult.
- Involve yourself in those activities which reduce anxiety.
- Learn and practise techniques for coping with maximum anxiety, e.g. panic.
- Learn skills of revising and taking examinations, e.g. how to set yourself manageable tasks and accomplish them within time limits.
- Learn relaxation techniques.
- Develop a balanced lifestyle.
- Ensure your need for sleep, appropriate diet, company, exercise and variety are met.
- Focus on tasks rather than yourself.
- Have a system for approaching problems and tasks.
- Write things down on paper rather than keeping them in your head.
- Form written hierarchies of difficulty, e.g. levels of anxiety; topics to be revised.
- Use others as helpers.
- Find out more about other helpful approaches, e.g. Yoga, Hypnosis.

# A checklist of techniques

| A Checklist of approaches, exercises and relaxation techniques for every potentially anxiety producing moment | Could I use this idea?<br>✓ = Yes<br>? = Not sure: Need to find out more about it<br>X = No | Tick when learnt<br>✓ | Page reference for relevant ideas and exercises |
|---|---|---|---|
| An emergency quick relaxation technique | | | 94 |
| *Thinking and Anxiety*<br>A self guidance Checklist to reduce stress | | | 79-81 |
| Exam 'Nerves': self statements to help you cope | | | 84-85 |
| Turning negative into positive self statements | | | 83 |
| Thought stopping | | | 81 |
| *Visualisation*<br>Create a scene in your imagination | | | 103 |
| A wave of relaxation through your body | | | 103 |
| Visualise taking the examination | | | 102 |
| A dream as a goal | | | 102 |
| *Muscular Relaxation*<br>A complete Do-it-Yourself Guide to Muscular Relaxation | | | 97 |
| When sitting at a desk | | | 101 |
| For your head and neck | | | 101 |
| Physical exercise | | | 90, 97 |
| *Breathing techniques*<br>The Complete Breath | | | 94-96 |
| Breathing Slowly and Deeply | | | 95 |
| Alternate Nostril Breathing | | | 96 |
| *Relaxation Exercises for different situations* when sitting at a desk | | | 101 |
| lying down | | | 93 |
| standing up | | | 94, 101 |
| sitting in a chair or on the floor | | | 97 |
| whilst revising | | | 101 |
| on the way to the exam room<br>in the exam room | | | 88, 95, 101 |
| *At different times of day*<br>Waking in the morning | | | 87 |
| On the morning before an afternoon exam | | | 88 |
| Getting to sleep at night | | | 89-92 |
| A good sleeping posture | | | 92 |

## Describing your past experience of examinations

It may help you pinpoint your past difficulties to answer these questions, either in the space provided or on a separate piece of paper:—

What has been your past experience of tests or exams? What kind of difficulties have you encountered?

Write down as many statements about yourself as possible which relate to any anxieties you have about taking examinations. It may help you to be specific by describing:

what you *thought* e.g. "I've not done enough work."

what you *felt* e.g. very nervous; panic.

how you *behaved* e.g. I got stomach aches; couldn't settle down to revision; lost sleep.

**Talking over the problem**

Having completed answering these questions, you may wish to talk over some issues with a helper. For suggestions see **Using Helpers.** You can also use the **Contents** and **Checklists** to seek answers to the problems you wish to overcome. You may, however, be feeling unclear about what problem to tackle or how to set about it, in which case the next exercise may help you clarify what you will do.

**Tackling the problem**

If you are feeling unclear about how to tackle a problem, the following four point action sequence may help you to get started.

---

(1)   State the *Problem* you wish to resolve:——
I want to
(This should be specific and contain an action verb e.g. write, list, run, etc.)

(2)   Set a *Goal*:
So that
(This should be a well-formed goal statement, clear and obtainable, stating what you wish to be like).

(3)   Determine an *Approach*
So I'm going to

(4)   Have a *Plan of action*
How I'm going to do it

---

**An example**

(1)   *I want to* learn emergency relaxation techniques.
(2)   *So that* I'm never going to 'freeze' or panic in an exam again.
(3)   *So I'm going to* learn 3 separate techniques i.e. **An Emergency Quick Relaxation Technique, Breathing Slowly and Deeply** and **Visualising the Examination.**
(4)   *How I'm going to do it* is to read the exercises, practise them by myself and then ask a friend to help me rehearse and practise them.

You can use a sheet of paper and the same sentence beginnings, "I want to . . ." etc., to construct your own action sequence, following the format above.

**A hierarchy of your anxiety**

It may help you to understand more clearly the causes of your anxiety to complete this exercise. Having done so, it will give you guidelines for which part of your anxiety to tackle first and subsequently.

### Draw up a list of situations that cause you anxiety

Try to be specific and detailed, sub-dividing the situations if they have a different scale of anxiety e.g. "Entering the Examination room" may subdivide into — meeting friends waiting outside; finding my seat; waiting for the invigilator to give instructions; turning over the question paper.

You may wish to use the space below or a separate sheet of paper.

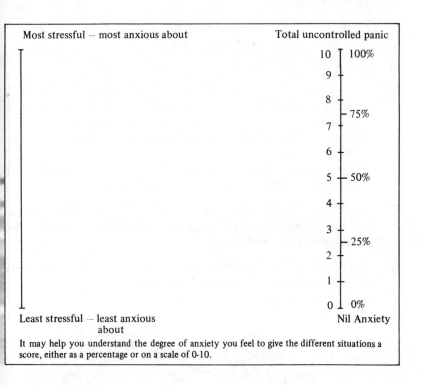

Most stressful — most anxious about

Total uncontrolled panic

10 — 100%
9
8
— 75%
7
6
5 — 50%
4
3
— 25%
2
1
0 — 0%

Least stressful — least anxious about

Nil Anxiety

It may help you understand the degree of anxiety you feel to give the different situations a score, either as a percentage or on a scale of 0-10.

### How to use the completed list

You have several choices.

(1)  You will probably find it easiest to start with situations at the 'least stressful' end of your list, particularly if they have a low anxiety score. You can then adopt one of two approaches.

Familiarise yourself thoroughly with that situation, simulating i.e. recreating as closely as possible, the situation that actually causes you stress, e.g. sitting at a desk in exam conditions; walking to the exam room; writing timed answers.

Use one of the relaxation techniques, e.g. **A Do it Yourself Guide to Muscular Relaxation.** Once you are in a state of complete relaxation, visualise the least stressful situation as ·vividly as possible. If you feel any anxiety or any tensing of muscles, then stop and return yourself to a complete state of relaxation again. If this happens at the beginning it means you have not sufficiently sub-divided your least stressful situation — you need a less stressful situation as a starting point.

Generally, you will not feel any tension as you visualise the first, least stressful situation. Having completed it, move on to visualising the second least stressful situation, and so on through your list. If at any point you feel tension you must:—

- Stop and return yourself to a state of total relaxation.
- Check to see if your list needs further sub-division; if there is a smaller anxiety step you can take. You will find you can take 2 or 3 steps at a time if this is going well. Don't rush it. Enjoy the state of relaxation and the gradual reduction of anxiety.
- You may find it helpful to use a friend as a helper with this exercise.
- You will no longer feel anxious about those situations you have visualised whilst in a state of complete relaxation.

(2) Learn and practise the exercises designed to cope with your most extreme anxiety, e.g. **An Emergency Quick Relaxation Technique, Breathing Slowly and Deeply.**

(3) Use the **Contents, Checklist,** your own questions, **The importance of asking questions,** and **Tackling the Problem** to help you proceed with other anxiety items on your list.

**Thinking and Anxiety:**
**A self-guidance checklist to reduce stress**

## How to use this checklist

1. Read through the whole page, noting points on the left hand side that apply to you.

2. Ensure you understand the list by checking any of the *Notes for guidance* that follow.

3. Select 1, 2 or 3 points on the right hand side that you can start to emphasise *immediately,* shifting the emphasis of your thinking from the left to the right hand side.

4. Note other points of relevance on the page. You may return to these on another occasion. Add this approach to any others you have for coping with anxiety.

| You are *MORE* likely to feel anxious when you think:— | You are *LESS* likely to feel anxious when you think:— | Tick (✓) the thinking approaches you will now take:— |
|---|---|---|
| * about the PAST | about the PRESENT, here and now | |
| * about the FUTURE, especially the long term future | about here and now, about the VERY NEXT THING YOU DO | |
| * NEGATIVE self statements | POSITIVE self statements | |
| * about YOURSELF | about TASKS: things you can achieve today | |
| * about WIDER or LARGER issues, concerns or tasks | about SPECIFIC issues, concerns or tasks | |
| * of SATISFYING others e.g. what other people will say | of SATISFYING yourself | |
| * about things YOU CANNOT DIRECTLY AFFECT even if you try | about things YOU CAN DIRECTLY AFFECT if you try | |
| * that you are UNABLE TO STOP YOURSELF THINKING ABOUT A CONCERN | that you are ABLE TO STOP YOURSELF THINKING ABOUT A PARTICULAR CONCERN | |
| * you are UNPREPARED | you are PREPARED | |
| * POSTPONE thinking or doing anything | you are going to take IMMEDIATE APPROPRIATE ACTION | |

These notes accompany **Thinking and Anxiety: a self guidance checklist to reduce stress.** They explain why certain patterns of thinking are less likely to cause you to feel stressed.

- You cannot do anything about the past. Worrying about a problem, difficulty or failure in the past gives it too great an emphasis in the PRESENT. You can do something about now.

- Thinking about the long-term failure can often feel daunting, even overwhelming. Thinking "What would happen to me if I fail" fuels anxiety and is counter-productive to success. Planning the short-term future, the VERY NEXT THING YOU DO, the next fifteen minutes, hour, evening, day, week, provides a useful manageable structure.

- Thinking about yourself; how you are feeling, how worried you are, your health, your career prospects, is one of the commonest forms of self-produced stress when studying. The need, when revising for and taking exams, is for you to be able to focus yourself effectively on TASKS, particularly those that are manageable and can be tackled immediately. The **Revision** section of the book is packed with suggestions as to how to do this effectively.

- The explanation for avoiding negative self-statements is contained in **Turning negative self-statements into positive self-statements.**

- When you say to yourself, "I must work tonight" or "I've got to get some revision done", you are likely to feel overwhelmed. Being highly SPECIFIC about issues, concerns or tasks gives you a manageable routine of activities. An example of an appropriate specific self-statement would be:
  "I am going to make a revision card on topic 'X', test myself on it during the next 30 minutes or so. I'll then make myself a drink and listen to one side of an L.P. before I tackle the next topic 'Y' in the same way".

- Even though we can often be more demanding of ourselves than others would be, it is generally more stressful to be thinking about what others expect of you, what they would say if you didn't get the grades or failed, etc. Fear of letting others down is a common form of exam anxiety and an enormous waste of emotional energy. SATISFYING YOURSELF and your own standards is a productive use of your energy.

- You cannot directly affect the examination system, the form it takes, the efficiency or justice of it or when you will take your examinations. Thinking about these is likely to leave you feeling out of control and relatively powerless. You can DIRECTLY AFFECT dozens of things about your life and study — this book is packed with suggestions of what and how — and these are going to help you feel more powerful and resourceful.

- If you are unable to stop yourself thinking about a concern it will certainly fuel your stress. You are ABLE TO STOP YOURSELF THINKING ABOUT A PARTICULAR CONCERN. Use **Turning negative self-statements into positive self-statements** as well as this self-guidance note to aid this process.

- If you are unprepared — don't know how to revise, have few stress coping techniques and don't know much about the examination procedure — you are certainly more likely to be stressed. You are doing something positive to be PREPARED by reading and using parts of this book.

- Postponing thinking about or doing something invariably fuels anxiety, increasing the intensity, occupying emotional energy unproductively. Taking IMMEDIATE APPROPRIATE ACTION like you are now by using this book is going to relieve these feelings.

## Thought Stopping

If you are having thoughts that worry you, try to say consistently to yourself "Stop" — you may wish to choose another *command word* that has more meaning to you e.g. your surname "Acres!" or something positive. "Think positive!" — as soon as you are aware of beginning to think or feel in a particular way. You can add to this some physical movement, like a click of your fingers to reinforce this command to yourself. You must be totally consistent if you adopt this approach. It may be hard work for the first day or so, but after that it will become a habit. This technique is usefully combined with **Turning negative self-statements into positive self-statements** i.e. saying "Stop" to yourself is followed by some positive statement about yourself, your intentions or your successes to date.

You can see the usefulness of thought stopping when you feel panic coming on. It is demonstrated in **An Emergency Quick Relaxation Technique.**

# Successful Exam Technique

David Cocker

Attractively laid out in self-contained spreads, this remarkably easy-to-use paperback breaks new ground for those thousands of students who want to develop a really winning revision and examination technique. With its quick reference headings, graphics, frequent checklists and summaries, it will be the one essential purchase for examination candidates throughout the English-speaking world, who want the help and want it fast.

CONTENTS
Understanding examinations, how to develop the right attitude, how to understand rules and regulations, past papers, the syllabus, types of questions, timing, marks, drawings, calculations, oral and practical examinations, marking schemes, the pass mark, how to deal with errors, results, appeals, how to use text and other books, how to organise studying and revision, how to face the examination room, how to answer the question, notes for parents, glossary, index.

DAVID COCKER BSc PhD CChem MRSC, a Post-Doctoral Fellow and University Demonstrator, has himself successfully sat some 100 main examination papers. This remarkable experience, coupled with his work as a tutor, invigilator and young examiner, has enabled him to develop and test a really comprehensive set of techniques, with students, now brought together in *Successful Exam Technique*.

96pp, 217 x 135mm. Illustrated. £2.95 paperback.
0 7463 0348 3.

Northcote House Publishers Ltd., Harper & Row House, Estover Road, Plymouth PL6 7PZ, United Kingdom. Tel: Plymouth (0752) 705251 Telex: 45635.

**Turning Negative self-statements into Positive self-statements**

Stress is often maintained by identifiable negative self-statements. *Below* in the left hand column are examples of negative self-statements. In the right hand column are examples of positive self-statements designed to replace them. Try to identify your own negative self-statements and write them in the blank spaces in the left hand column. Then, using the positive examples above as a guideline, construct your own positive self-statements. Abandon all negative self-statements and put your energy into positive self-statements.

| Negative statements | Positive statements |
|---|---|
| I can't concentrate | My concentration has really improved. Even when it lapses I know how to recover it. |
| I can't cope. | I can cope and I'm going to do so. |
| Everyone seems to be doing more work than I am. | Other people are irrelevant – its the quality of my learning that matters and I now have the techniques to do my work well. |
| I might fail. I am going to fail. What if I fail . . .? I won't be able to face 'X' again . . . | I intend to pass, I'm doing a lot to ensure that happens and I can only do my best. That's what I intend to do. |
| I'm in a mess with my revision. I'll never be able to do enough or catch up. I don't know where to start. | I can get my work done in time when I plan a proper *revision timetable, decide priorities* and know *how to revise* efficiently. |
| I always make a mess of exams. I've never been able to do well at exams. | The past is irrelevant. I'm now working well and have learnt the techniques to do well in these exams – a new beginning. |
|  |  |
|  |  |
|  |  |
|  |  |
|  |  |
|  |  |

**Exam 'Nerves': Self Statements to help you cope**

One way of managing your 'nerves', that is your anxiety or even panic, is to learn by heart.

In the following four situations choose those statements which you can say convincingly to yourself either silently or out loud.

At first, you may find it difficult to say any statement convincingly to yourself. In which case, follow this sequence:—

● Choose one of two from the existisng list .or add your own.

● Make the statement *real* and realistic to you. Alter it so it remains positive but feels like something you could say to yourself.

● Practise saying it to yourself, regularly. You are aiming for it to become a well engrained habit to say these statements to yourself rather than the old negative, worrying statements.

● Once you have mastered one or two, add others, expanding your list of useful self-statements, following the same system as above.

**The Self Statements**
Other action you can take is in brackets.

*Preparing for my exams*
What is it I have to do?
(Extract all the parts for you from the examination techniques and anxiety coping sections of this book.)

I'm going to plan what to do about my anxiety and not waste time being anxious.

I'm going to think positively — no negative self-statements.
(See other ideas in **Thinking and Anxiety: a self guidance checklist to reduce stress.**)

I'm not going to get involved in conversations I don't want.
(Keep conversations that may be anxiety-provoking, brief and manageable.)

I'm going to be ready for anything that happens to me.

If the worst happens I'm not going to be thrown into a panic — I'll learn how to cope.
(See, for example, **An Emergency Quick Relaxation Technique.**)

It will be different this time, I know how to cope.

*During the exam itself*
Now's my chance to put into action what I've learned.
Stick to the here-and-now.
What is the very next thing I'm going to do?
It's different this time — I know how to cope.
I can handle me *and* the tasks.
I can reason and/or relax my fear away.
I need some anxiety: I'll make what I feel work *for* me.
(You do! It's a stimulus to coping, awareness, etc.)
Relax, I'm in control. Take a slow, deep breath.
Great. This gives me the chance to show what I know, think, believe, understand, can do, etc.

*Coping with the feeling of being overwhelmed*
Stop! I can manage this panic: it's no different from any other situation — use the exercises!

When fear comes, just pause.
Stick to here-and-now: What is the very next thing I'm going to do?
I could expect my fear to rise at times. Don't try to eliminate the fear, just keep it manageable.
Label my fear from 0 to 10 and watch it change.

*Looking back on the experience*
What an achievement.
There'll always be something I could have done better but I've really done well.
It's a great feeling.
I'm really making progress.
I managed my fear.
It wasn't as bad as I expected.
I've done it.
Wait until I tell . . .
(fill in the name of someone important you'd really want to tell.)

**Situations and Stress**

How you think, feel or behave can be reinforced by being back in the same immediate environment, in the same place or same situation, e.g. being in the same room, house, library or with the same people around you.

Here are approaches you can take to cope with stress related to situations.

(1) *For situations that cannot be avoided* and yet cause you to feel stressed, *learn and practise the relaxation ideas* in this section. You can come to feel better feelings about people and places by adopting a calmer, more positive, more relaxed approach.

Where your anxiety is related to unknown or unfamiliar situations e.g. the exam room, then try to *simulate* the situation as closely as possible e.g. if your anxiety is about where you are going to take the exam, then find the room in advance, enter it when you are able to do so, get the feel of being in it in a quiet atmosphere. (See also **Getting used to Examinations.**)

(2) *Avoid those situations that cause you stress that are avoidable.* Identify the situations you find stressful. You may wish to list them below or on a separate sheet of paper.

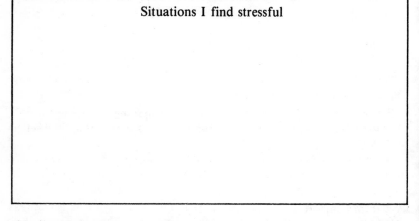

Situations I find stressful

Once identified you may wish to use a helper to talk over what you could do to avoid or minimise the stress involved in these situations. **Tackling the Problem** may also be a useful aid.

(3) *Alter what you are doing in these situations* to minimise the stress. For example, if where you are revising is causing you stress, you may be able to improve the furniture arrangement. Moving a piece of furniture so that you get a better view, more natural daylight or enough heat is one approach. Arranging books, files, papers, pens and equipment so that they are accessible around you would be another approach.

(4) Make a point of *placing yourself in those situations that make you feel good,* relaxed, purposeful, as often as you are able to do so. You may wish to list them below or on a separate sheet of paper.

```
┌─────────────────────────────────────────────────────────────┐
│               Situations in which I feel good                 │
│                                                               │
│                                                               │
│                                                               │
│                                                               │
│                                                               │
│                                                               │
└─────────────────────────────────────────────────────────────┘
```

(5) *Vary* where you are and who you are with to give yourself the stimulus of a change in environment.

Although establishing an effective routine can help both to complete tasks and to work in a composed and effective manner, it may at times leave you feeling unstimulated, bored, jaded.

(6) *Balancing* a day, or a week or a weekend between tasks, places, people, work, recreation, exercise, diet, sleep and entertainment is a very important skill in maximising the effectiveness of your study.

## Waking up in the morning

There are times during revision when you can feel jaded when waking. Apart from washing and showering, these ideas may help.

**Paddle in cold water.**    Walking up and down in 1 or 2 inches of water in a bath for a minute or two. Not as painful as a cold shower but refreshing, stimulating!

**Bare foot walk.**    A walk in bare feet on paving stones or grass, even with the dew rising, for a few minutes. Walk slowly, steadily, feeling the ground under your feet. This is refreshing and stimulating.

**Physical exercises.**    A jog, run, brisk walk or swim are all potentially stimulating at the beginning of a day. Your circulation can equally well be stimulated by stepping up on to a chair, and stepping down again, between 5 and 10 times, or any similar exercises, such as those contained in the Canadian Air Forces XBX exercises. All these physical pursuits need to be appropriate to your health, fitness and age to aid your alertness rather than decrease it!

**The Complete Breath.**    This is a version of the simple Yoga exercise, described in Richard Hittleman's useful book, 'Yoga for Health'. It is included in **Breathing Techniques.**

## The morning before an afternoon exam

- Prepare a free morning before an afternoon exam in advance. By the evening before, know how you are going to spend the time, dividing it into half an hour and, if appropriate, quarter of an hour units.
- Plan into the morning some relaxation, exercise or quiet, low key entertainment, e.g. listening to music.
- *Don't attempt any new revision topics* — Attempting to learn *new* topics at this late stage can affect your recall of those topics you already know and/or understand well.
- Use any *key word cards* or notes you have, not great bulky files, simply to recall and recheck your understanding, asking questions to which you will provide answers, without looking at the card. This simulates the exam conditions.
- For a paper involving mathematics or problem-solving, practise your recall of methods or formula for more familiar questions.
- Plan into the morning when and what you are going to eat and drink. Try to eat something of nutritional value, but watch your liquid intake — many exams are 2 or 3 hours long!
- Incorporate all the relevant ideas from **On the way to the exam**.

## On the way to the exam

You will maximise your effectiveness in examinations if you organise the time immediately before an examination. It will also enable you to minimise your anxiety. Some or all of the following ideas will also help.

- Minimise your waiting time outside an exam room, know the location of the room and time your walk, rehearsing it if necessary. You may either come direct from your home or find a temporary waiting place, near the exam room that you can use until a few minutes before the examination.
- Meet only those people you want to meet, if any. Agree with friends not to stand around before the exam making anxiety-provoking conversation, e.g. about how nervous you are feeling; what topics you have revised or questions you think are going to be on the paper. Avoid waiting around outside altogether or talking to anybody, if you wish, by timing your arrival so that you can walk straight into the room a few minutes before the exam is due to start.
- Practise your rehearsed self-statements. Keep them positive. You are ready to go.
- Practise your breathing, visualising, muscular and/or Emergency Quick Relaxation techniques both to keep your composure and as practice in the event of their being needed.

## Getting to sleep at night

If you are finding it hard to fall asleep at night or are waking early, there are several approaches you can take. Select those which have most appeal to you, are most available and possible.

## Causes of sleep loss

A first approach is to *cope with any anxiety* you are feeling *about the disrupted sleep pattern*. You can almost certainly lose sleep for short periods of time without the loss having a profound effect upon you. Some of the anxiety coping techniques in this section of the book can be used to help you cope with any such anxiety.

You may, of course, be deliberately cutting down on sleep to cram in more revision and study time. You can keep a check on whether this sleep loss is adversely affecting your study effectiveness by *self-monitoring*.

Ask yourself:—

— Are you being agitated, upset or angered by small incidents?
— Is your concentration noticeably deteriorating, both by 'not being able to take anything in' or not being able to recall something you have just read or done?
— Are you feeling emotionally overwhelmed by all the tasks?
— Do you lack energy and/or appetite?

If the answer to some of these questions is 'YES', then it is likely that your need for sleep (or proper diet, exercise, company, entertainment or relaxation, which are also considered in this section of the book) is not being met.

## Experiencing a sense of achievement

If you have completed a task, no matter how small, you are likely to be able to rest easier. Use the techniques in the **Revision** section of the book to help with this.

## Watch what you eat and drink

Avoid indigestible food, excessive liquid and stimulants such as too much or too strong coffee. Alcohol needs to be monitored as well. Whilst a small quantity can act as a relaxant and decrease your alertness, large quantities will act as a depressant and reduce your ability to achieve or rest easily.

## Take exercise

Walks, jogs, runs, swims, a game of squash, an exercise programme, are all familiar, appropriate examples. Being physically tired, even exhausted, does certainly help you sleep. Studying is often a very physically passive business: it needs to be broken up with activity and a change of scenery.

### Exercises and postures

Use relaxation exercises or postures, illustrated and explained in this book. Practise them, working at a good, relaxed, sleeping posture. See **A good sleeping posture**

### Recall the day — in reverse

When in a relaxed sleep posture, try, as an alternative to counting sheep, recalling the events of the day moment-by-moment in detail. However, do it backwards i.e. starting from the very last thing you did before you got into bed. Hopefully you won't get as far as recalling when you woke up.

### The need for entertainment

*Meet your need for entertainment,* for a break from study. Think about what causes you to enjoy yourself, relax and take your mind fully away from study. The list of possible activities is endless. The following are some examples students have mentioned to me during the course of one term:—

> playing a guitar, listening to music on headphones, writing songs and poems, watching films, taking photographs, going to discos, going to the pub, cooking a meal for friends

### Enjoy the close company of others

A close friendship or friendships involving the ability to share intimacies, be open, being yourself is immensely valuable at any time and particularly at times of pressure.

### Use Water

Water is very therapeutic. Warm baths or showers can be excellent relaxants immediately before going to bed, as can swimming. I use these a lot for relaxation.

### Saunas and Massage

If you have access to a Sauna or you know anybody who can offer a skilled massage, both are excellent relaxants prior to sleep.

### Go to bed at a time you are ready for sleep

You may be familiar with the idea of 'biological clocks', i.e. that everybody has a natural rhythm, a sequence of ups and downs (cycles) that affect their alertness, need for sleep, mood and other aspects of their being. Whether or not you understand or accept the idea, there seems to me to be no doubt that there are differences in both the amount of sleep people need and the time they need to go to sleep.

My experience is that some people need to get to bed early after completing their study in the early evening, whilst others can work very effectively late at night, studying to midnight and beyond. In general, those in early or mid-teens seem less able to study late into the night than those in late teens or older age groups, but there will be exceptions. If you have developed an effective means of *self-monitoring* yourself, like that on p.36 you can prevent yourself from *attempting* to work beyond your productive limits. Try to be honest with yourself. If you know it is your anxiety that is keeping you up and your concentration, understanding and retention is poor, you are wasting time that could be valuably used the next day for study.

Likewise, there is no point in going to bed to try to sleep when you don't feel like sleep. Use the time more constructively, more creatively (as suggested above). Further, there seems little point in lying in bed worrying about not sleeping. You would be better occupied doing something which caused you less stress:— making yourself a drink; listening to music on headphones; tackling a small, yet niggling, study task; using one of the relaxation exercises.

### Someone to talk to
Seek out those people to whom you can talk with confidence. Those who will listen attentively, not moralise, keep confidentiality and help yourself to put things in perspective. Take this book along. Use it together, selecting the ideas which best suit you.

If your lack of sleep continues it may be advisable to visit your doctor. There is no clear cut guideline on how long you should tolerate disruption of sleep before seeking help, although between one and three weeks would seem appropriate.

A good sleeping posture is *illustrated* below.

Lie on your right side, drawing up your bent left leg so that it comes comfortably to rest alongside your waist area. Your right leg stretches out straight.

Allow your right arm to lie straight alongside your right side, whilst your left arm is bent. Your head should by supported by a pillow or pillows.

You may prefer to try this on your left side or make small alterations to the position of your arms and legs.

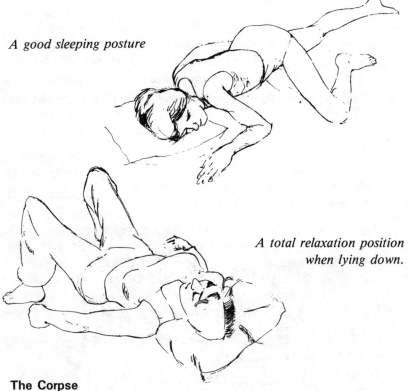

*A good sleeping posture*

*A total relaxation position when lying down.*

### The Corpse

The objective of the Corpse is to be able to completely relax every muscle in your face and body. Anxiety will lessen when you relax muscles.

It involves lying on the floor, a bed, in or on a sleeping bag, pillows or cushions and is a position that encourages deep relaxation and sleep. Wear comfortable, loose clothing and dispense with shoes.

# Sleeping posture

- Lie down slowly on your back with your arms by your sides.

- Allow your arms to come to rest with your hands a few inches away from your body and palms upwards, curling your fingers if they want to do so.

- Your feet should be allowed to fall open, spreading outwards, until they settle in a comfortable position a few inches apart.

- Raise your chin 6 to 8 cm. (2 inches or so), tilting your head backwards so that your eyes are facing directly above you, then close your eyes.

- Try to let all your muscles become limp and heavy. Let your facial muscles go, your arms and legs become floppy and heavy, settling into a comfortable, still posture.

- Inhale deeply and slowly to enable your whole breathing to slow down with each intake of breath, don't take another breath until you have to do so. Simply concentrate your attention on your breathing and nothing else.

- You may stay in this position for any length of time. When you have finished, rise very slowly to avoid dizziness, raising yourself into a sitting or semi-upright position on your right side before eventually standing.

**A total relaxation position when lying down**

Initially, lie as in the position for **The Corpse.** There are two differences as you can see in the *illustration*. The first is that you raise your knees, so that they are firmly and comfortably supported by your feet on the ground. The knees should be between approximately 12 cm. and 30 cm. (6 to 12 inches) apart.

The second difference is that you raise your head 5 to 8 cm. (2 to 3 inches) by resting the back on a thick book or books or a cushion. As with the Corpse, raise your chin by tilting your head back 5 cm. (2 inches) or so.

You may then close your eyes, breathing slowly and deeply as in the Corpse.

As with the Corpse you may continue in the position, which enables the base of your spine to be very comfortable supported, as long as you wish or time permits. Rise, as in all such exercises, very slowly, sitting up first then slowly rising to your feet.

This is a lovely relaxing position, for a few minutes or a longer period of time.

Learning how to breathe more fully and appropriately by using one or more of these four exercises is another very helpful approach to removing tension and refreshing yourself.

### An Emergency Quick Relaxation Technique

This exercise is to counteract panic and the build up of tension. It is adapted from Jane Madders useful book 'Stress and Relaxation'.

1) Say sharply to yourself 'STOP' (aloud if the situation permits).
2) Breathe in and hold your breath for a moment before *slowly* exhaling. As you do so relax your shoulders and hands. (See also **A Do-it-Yourself Guide to Muscular Relaxation**).
3) Pause for a moment, then as you breathe in slowly again, relax your forehead and jaw.
4) Stay quiet for a few moments then go on with what you were doing, moving slowly and smoothly.
5) If you have to talk, speak a little more slowly and with your voice a little lower then usual.

This STOP! relaxation can usually be done without anybody noticing and you will find that, in spite of your feelings, the tension will lessen.

### The Complete Breath

The essential feature of this exercise is that everything is completed SLOWLY.

(1) Stand upright with your arms by your side. Exhale. (see Figure 1).

(2) Breathe in through your nose. As you do so, inhale, filling as fully as possible your stomach/abdomen area first and thereafter your chest (see Figure 2).

(3) *At the same time,* bring your arms above your head and rise on to your toes.
Hold this for a moment (see Figure 3).

(4) Breathe out through your nose, expelling the air from your abdomen through your chest. As you do so, lower your arms to your sides and your feet to the floor again.

You can repeat this between 3 and 10 times. If you wish you can count to 8 as you inhale and do the same as you exhale. Alternatively, you can start to raise yourself onto the balls of your feet when your arms reach the horizontal half way point of their journey to above your head, lowering yourself onto your heels slowly from the halfway point of their journey down.

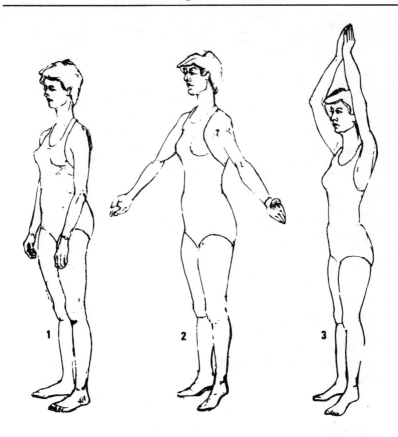

## Breathing Slowly and Deeply

The same sequence illustrated in **The Complete Breath** can be used at any time, without the accompanying stretching movements. It is useful to avoid the build up of tension, or to reduce it once it has occurred. The sequence is as follows:—

(1) Breathe in slowly through your nose to the count of 8. As you inhale the air, imagine you are filling your stomach/abdomen area first and thereafter your chest.

(2) Hold this breath in for as long as it remains comfortable to do so.

(3) Expel the air slowly through your nose to the count of 8, expelling the air from your abdomen upwards through your chest.

(4) Refrain from taking another intake of breath until it becomes uncomfortable and repeat the sequence 1 to 4, again.

Three times is usually enough to reduce the level of tension and to refresh you. You may extend this if you need to do so.

It is a useful technique for the exam room.

## Alternate Nostril Breathing

This is an effective relaxant that can help with tension and head congestion.

Inhale through the right nostril, closing the left nostril with the thumb of your left hand. Count slowly to 4 as you inhale.

Close both nostrils with your left thumb and forefinger and hold your breath to the slow count of 4.

Exhale through your left nostril to the slow count of 4, whilst closing your right nostril with your forefinger (or first two fingers whichever you find easier).

Release both nostrils, remaining without breath for another count of 4.

Repeat, breathing in through the left nostril.

Once you have established an even 4-4-4-4 routine and can complete the thumb and forefinger movements easily, close your eyes when doing this exercise.

You can try variations on this 4-4-4-4 routine. Try *in* for 6, count to 3; *out* for 6, count to 3; *in* for 6, etc. 8/4/8/4 combinations, once you're used to the others, will slow and deepen your breathing even more. You can practise this exercise for 5 minutes or so at a time — even three or four sequences will be beneficial.

The basic principle involved in muscular relaxation is that when muscles are tensed really hard and then relaxed, the muscles will go into a deeper state of relaxation than formerly. When your muscles are relaxed in this

way *you cannot be in a state of tension* — the two states are not compatible. In such a composed physical state you are going to be able to study more effectively, and be mentally alert with the negative effects of anxiety behind you.

You can achieve muscular relaxation as an *after-effect from strenuous physical exertion* such as running, squash, swimming, squat thrusts and team ball games. Such exertion will cause you to *breathe more deeply and fully* and this will also contribute to your more relaxed state afterwards. There are obvious differences in fitness and overall health that determine what exercise is appropriate to you; how much exercise; how often and for how long. A marathon run is not generally an appropriate starting point for most people! Physical Education teachers, the Health Education Council's 'Look after Yourself' materials and courses as well as medical opinion are all available for you to consult if you are in doubt about what is appropriate for you.

In addition, the following exercises will give you practice of muscular relaxation.

A Do it Yourself Guide to Muscular Relaxation
Exercises to use when sitting at a desk
An exercise for relaxing your head and neck

## A 'Do It Yourself' Guide to Muscular Relaxation

Relaxation of individual muscle groups or the whole body is a skill which everyone can learn and which improves with practice. It is important to be able to recognise muscle tension and then to release this tension at will. It is only when this skill has been learned that the full benefits of muscular relaxation during anxious and stressful situations can be achieved.

The following programme involves tensing and then relaxing the main muscle groups of the body in turn. Ideally, each group should be tensed and the tension released *three times* in succession:—

first of all tensing the muscles as tightly as possible
secondly with moderate tension
finally with minimal tension

It may help you to *count to 5 slowly and silently* on each of these three tensings. This helps us to recognise the muscle tension which is part of our reaction to stress, and the contrasting feel of muscles which are relaxed.

The best way to learn the skill of relaxation is to find a friend who will *slowly* talk you through the following programme. If this is not possible, read through the programme and learn the order of muscles to be relaxed and then work through from memory or from a *key word card*.

# Your relaxation programme

| Part of the body (key words) | Instructions (Repeat each movement three times) | What you will feel (Helpers read this aloud after the Instructions) |
|---|---|---|
| *Start* with the face | | |
| *Forehead*<br>Raise eyebrows | Raise your eyebrows and frown heavily, with maximum tension<br>*Repeat* with moderate and minimal tension | Feel the tension across the forehead and scalp. Release the tension and feel the forehead become smooth and the muscles relax |
| *Eyes and Nose*<br>Screw up eyes | Screw your eyes up tightly | Feel the tension spreading over the whole of your face and the contrasting calm, soothing feeling as the tension is released |
| *Mouth and Jaw*<br>Clench teeth | Clench your teeth together firmly to tense the jaw muscles | Feel the tension around the jaw and throat. Release the tension and let your jaw muscles become loose letting your mouth hang open if it wishes |
| Ear-to-ear grin | Tense the muscles around the mouth by smiling in an exaggerated way — an ear to ear grin — then let the smile fade away | Feel the muscles relax |
| Tongue | Tense the tongue by pressing it firmly against the back of the teeth. Slowly release and let the tongue rest in the mouth | Feel the release of tension and the tongue relaxing in your mouth |
| *Forearms*<br>Wrist back — hand forward | Bend your wrist back and push forward hard with your hand | As you let the tension go, feel warm, tingling sensation of relaxed muscles in the forearms |
| *Upper arms*<br>Bend elbows | Bend both arms at the elbow. Flex the biceps really firmly, slowly relax these muscles | Feel the heaviness in your arms spread down to your finger tips |
| *Shoulders and Chest*<br>Hands and arms at side | Press your hands and the arms firmly against the side of your body. Press really hard and then release the tension and let your shoulders hang loose | Your arms will feel heavy and relaxed again |

| Part of the body (key words) | Instructions (Repeat each movement three times) | What you will feel (Helpers read this aloud after the Instructions) |
| --- | --- | --- |
| *Neck and Back* | | |
| Chin out | Jut your chin out in front of you or, if you are lying down, raise your head about one inch from the ground | Feel the tension in your neck muscles and its release as you bring your head down to a comfortable resting position |
| Chin in | Draw your chin in towards your neck or, if lying down, press your head back into the floor. Hold it briefly, then release | Feel tension building in your neck, shoulders and back<br><br>Enjoy the contrasting feel of the muscles as they relax and lose the tension |
| Neck stretch | Elongate your neck and feel the tension until it is released | Feel the tension until it is released and slowly subsides |
| Retract neck | Retract your neck by shortening your neck as much as possible | Feel the tension and slowly release it |
| Shrug shoulders | Try and touch your ears with your shoulders then let them slump back | Feel a heavy relaxed feeling once more which is spreading through your upper body |
| Shoulder blades | Draw your shoulder blades firmly together | Feel the tightness created then relax the muscles and let your shoulders slump |
| Arched back | Hollow your back by arching it more and more. Relax back into chair or on to floor | Feel the support that the chair or floor offers |
| *Stomach, Thighs and Buttocks* | | |
| Pull in stomach | Pull your stomach muscles in tighter and tighter, then let go. | Feel warmth and tingling feelings at it is released. |
| Heels against floor | With feet flat on the floor, pull the heels backwards against the resistance of the floor, tightening all the muscles at the back of the thighs. Relax these muscles. With feet still flat on the floor press the heels down firmly into the floor and let the muscles relax completely. | Feel the difference when the tension is released |
| Buttocks | Tighten muscles in your buttocks and release | Feel the release of tension that this produces |
| *Calves and Feet* | | |
| Point toes | Point your toes, extending the ankle joint. Then let the ankle become loose and the muscles relaxed | Feel the tension in the muscles at the back of the lower leg |
| Toes up | Flex the ankle by bending the toes up towards the knee | Feel the tension build again. Feel the warm, tingling feeling of relaxation spread down your legs |
| Curl toes | Curl your toes up tightly then release this tension 3 times | With the strain released, let the toes rest naturally |
| Stretch toes | Stretch your toes out strongly as far as you can | As the feet relax completely let the soothing, heavy feeling in your legs spread to the tips of your toes |

## Time required

At first it will take approximately 20 to 30 minutes to go through the entire procedure properly. With practice you will be able to become quite relaxed in 10 to 15 minutes.

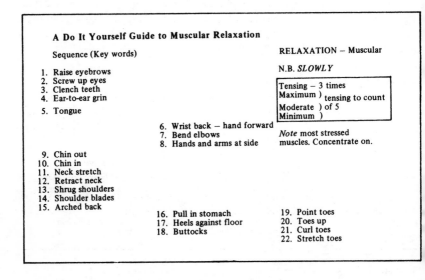

An alternative is to buy a commercially produced relaxation programme on audio-tape. More details of some programmes are included in **Further reading and help**. Yet another alternative is to record your own audio-tape, using this programme.

Like any other skill (driving a car, playing the piano) it will need practice, but the benefits can be enormous, and it is enjoyable to do in itself!

## The Relaxation Programme

*Preparing yourself*

Just settle back in a chair and find a position where you are comfortable. Let the chair support your body weight. Let your hands rest on your lap and have your head comfortably balanced on your neck and shoulders. (If you prefer, lie down flat on the floor or on a bed with your legs stretched out. Let your arms lie loosely alongside your body, as in **The Corpse**, palms turned down, or if it is more comfortable have your hands resting across you abdomen). Now close your eyes. Sigh to release tension. Pay attention to the rhythm of your own breathing. Breathe out a little more deeply. Feel your abdomen rise as you breathe in and as you exhale feel your whole body sink into the chair, letting all your muscles relax. Pause for a while.

**You are now in a state of total relaxation**

Concentrate on the rhythm of your own breathing as you sit/lie in total relaxation. Think of all the muscles you have just relaxed and feel them sinking into a deeper state of relaxation. In times of stress, muscle tension can manifest itself in different parts of the body — e.g. the clenched fist, the furrowed brow, the aching neck and shoulders — so *concentrate particularly on the muscle groups which reflect your anxiety and tension* and register the way they feel in this relaxed state.

**Ending the relaxation programme**

When you are ready to end this period of relaxation come round very slowly. Just wiggle your toes and fingers a little when you are ready, have a stretch and open your eyes. You should feel refreshed and calm, ready to face the demands of your daily life.

**Exercises to use when sitting at a desk during examinations or revision**

These isometric exercises involve some of the same principles involved in **A Do it Yourself Guide to Muscular Relaxation.**

| | |
|---|---|
| Pull in stomach muscles tightly hold for count of 5 Relax | Grasp below seat of chair pull up for count of 5 Relax |
| Clench fist tightly hold for count of 5 Relax | Press elbows tightly into side of body hold for count of 5 Relax |
| Extend fingers hold for a count of 5 Relax | Push foot hard into floor hold for count of 5 Relax |

**An Exercise for relaxing your head and neck**

Allow your head to DROP forward. Try not to pull it down. You should feel muscles at back of your neck being stretched by the weight of your head. Repeat, allowing your head to drop backward, then to the left and right.

A selection of the above exercises will only take about 30 seconds and can be most helpful to relieve the strain (or even cramp) which occurs when sitting writing at a desk during an examination. Performed between questions or sections of an exam, the exercises may also aid in 'switching off' from one topic and focussing on the next.

Creating a picture in your mind or *visualisation* has at least *four uses* when studying for exams. Use the same upward eye movements as described in **Use your eyes for visual recall** (p.44).

(1) Its use has been explained in *remembering* and in constructing key word revision cards in the **Revision** section.

(2) At fourteen years of age, Duncan Goodhew, a future swimming champion determined he was going to go to the Olympics. It was his target, his goal throughout the years of hard training. He imagined how it would be, the race, what it would feel like afterwards and this dream drove him on and sustained him over the years. This use of *a dream as a goal* is well known to many sportsmen and women. They are aware that it is not just ability, technique, determination or hard work that create success, but an extra key factor within the person. It is not always clear what this is, but a dream is certainly one such factor.
*Constructing your own dream,* visualising what you intend to achieve for yourself, could become a powerful motivating force for you in your study.

(3) *Visualise taking the examination*
Use one of the relaxation exercises to bring yourself into a composed, comfortable and relaxed state.
Now imagine yourself in the same composed, calm state taking the examination
You feel purposeful and confident. You see yourself at a desk, in the exam room environment. You feel entirely at home and attuned to that moment, working effectively and concentrating well.
Practise visualising this positive, clear, realistic image over and over again.

(4) *Visualising as a relaxation technique*
**Create a scene in your imagination** and **A wave of relaxation through your body** are two exercises using the visualisation principle, and **Imagining your limbs feeling warm and heavy** is another, using what you have learned about **Muscular relaxation.**

**Create a scene in your imagination**

The ability to create a scene in your imagination as a place to retreat into when stress is near can be very useful.

- Think of a scene or a moment in time in your mind. It can be real or imaginary; from the past, present or future.
- The essential features of this scene are that it creates within you *pleasant feelings of safety, warmth, security, peace.*
- It must be unaffected by bad messages, uneasy thoughts, painful memories.
- In your imagination create as *vivid* a scene as possible. *Picture* the scene, the colours, the movement in the scene, the precise detail. *Hear* the sounds associated with the scene in the same kind of detail. *Feel* the touch experiences associated with the moment such as temperature; wind; the feel of your body; anything you touched. Add to these any *tastes* or *smells* associated with the moment.
- It may take you a little time to construct such a scene. You may choose to have more than one. Practise recalling this scene several times when not feeling stressed. With practice it can be very quickly brought to mind. It can only take a few seconds, or at most a minute or two, to dwell in this lovely imagined world. You can then quickly return to present reality in a more composed state.

You can use this technique in any situation, e.g. an exam room, standing around waiting for something to happen. It is not visible to other people, except perhaps by the peaceful look on your face.

In learning it, however, you may find it helpful to sit in a comfortable chair or lie on a bed and use other relaxation exercises such as breathing or muscular relaxation before it.

**A wave of relaxation through your body**

- Sit comfortably in a chair or lie in a comfortable position.
- Close your eyes and imagine yourself to be transparent and filled with your favourite colour of liquid. Imagine it to be exactly at the temperature you find comfortable. If you are unsure of a colour, choose some variation of blue, e.g. turquoise or aquamarine.
- Starting from the crown of your head, imagine this liquid draining slowly away down your body. As it does so, imagine each part of the body from which it has drained feeling lighter and relieved of tension. Imagine the liquid eventually flowing out through the tips of your fingers and toes and you'll be left feeling relaxed.
  Repeat if necessary. Move only slowly when you first rise, to avoid dizziness.

**More exercises**

### Imagining your limbs feeling warm and heavy

Once you are aware of how muscles feel when they are relaxed and you have used your imagination to develop a composed state of mind, you can combine these two approaches in this exercise.

Lying down or sitting comfortably, imagine your limbs to be feeling very heavy. It may help you to close your eyes for a while and focus upon one part of the body at a time, e.g. your right hand; lower arm; upper arm.

Once all the limbs feel heavy, imagine a feeling of warmth in all these limbs. Exclude from this your neck area (where tension is often to be found). Imagine your neck to feel cool and light.

With practice this exercise only takes a few minutes and can be used in an upright sitting posture in the exam room.

### Focussed Listening

This exercise complements the **Visualise taking the exam** exercise in that it helps focus attention and concentration in the exam room. In addition, it is a relaxation exercise in its own right. The object of the exercise is to develop your ability to listen to only those sounds you wish to hear and thus be more discriminating in your listening. Thus if potentially disruptive sounds occur in or outside the exam room you will continue to maintain your concentration. A window cleaner whistling; a lawn mower working outside (quite a common occurrence this in summer exams); building or road works; another candidate taken ill are examples of situations that you will be able to take in your stride.

---

The exercise
Spend around 60 seconds,
- listening to sounds outside the room you are in, e.g. sounds of traffic, birds, rain or wind, voices, footsteps on stairs.

Another 60 seconds
- listening to sounds in the room, e.g. a radiator clinking, the movement of a chair, a clock ticking, a cough.

Another 60 seconds
- listening to the sounds *immediately around* you and within you, e.g. breathing, the movement of your paper and pen, the sound of clearing your throat, your chair.

It is this third — emphasised — listening that you wish to be able to develop and use in the exam room, excluding the sounds in the room and beyond.

Practice being able to focus on your immediate environment in this way as an aid to your concentration.

# 5

# Using others as Helpers

**Introduction**

This section gives guidelines to *both students and their helpers* (other students, friends, parents, spouses and others).

Throughout, it emphasises the importance of *negotiating help* with another person. That is, *not demanding* it *or forcing it upon others* but *requesting* and *offering*. In practical terms, this means that the helper asks questions like:

'Is there anything I can do to help?'

It also means that the student asks questions like:

'Could you help me with . . .?'

It also means that the answer to both these questions could be 'No', at least initially, and that the times and conditions for help have to be discussed. Helpers can state clearly what they are prepared to offer in the way of help. Students can state equally clearly their needs (when they know what they are); helpers can help them discover their needs where they are unclear.

**Helpful and unhelpful things for helpers to say**

I have asked students which things their parents, friends or other helpers say which are most helpful and which are most unhelpful. They say:

---

**Unhelpful**                                    **Do you agree?**

It's not worth worrying about.
Cheer up.
Have you finished yet?
Pull yourself together.
You've just got to get down to it/
You must get down to it.
Get a grip on yourself.
Do some work and you'll feel better.
You can only do your best.
Don't worry.
It will be all right on the day.
Have you done your home work tonight?
Your brother/sister/cousin/friend/etc.
never had this problem . . .
Others . . .

**Helpful**                                       **Do you agree?**

Is there anything I can do to help?
How's it going?
Do you want any help with anything?
How are you feeling about things?
Let me know if I can help in any way.
You seem to be working hard/You are
finding it difficult to get down to it . . .
I'll test you on that topic if you want.
Others . . .

## Features of these comments and questions

They tend to be open questions, offering, without forcing, help. They accept the student's feelings.

- You may find some items in 'Unhelpful' list, helpful and vice versa. It does not matter. *It is important* that you *negotiate with your helper(s)* so that they know what is helpful to you and what is not.

## Working with fellow students and friends

In the early days of schooling, you may often have felt as if you were cheating if you worked with other students on the same question. Working with others can be immensely useful, of course, and the following guidelines are designed to ensure the maximum usefulness.

- Work on each other's strengths i.e. the topics you know best, are most interested in, etc.
- Constructively support each other by listening attentively; telling friends when they have been helpful; avoiding anxiety-provoking topics.
- Co-operate. Use any competitiveness to the benefit of all rather than the detriment of individuals. Don't try to elevate your own self-confidence at the expense of others (you will find fellow students who try this at exam time).
- Make group decisions binding on each member of the group. If you have voluntarily, without being placed under any duress, agreed to do something, you must answer to the group if you have not done so.
- Form groups to practise particular techniques e.g. *relaxation techniques; visualisation* for relaxation. Meet regularly and help each other.

## Guidelines for helpers

- Work through the book yourself, familiarising yourself, in particular, with the parts that are of direct interest and concern to the student.
- Work through the book with the student, agreeing which parts.
- Try to avoid imposing your own anxieties on to the student when the student is feeling anxious. Discuss these *either* with another person *or* with the student when the student is less anxious and wants to listen *or* both.
- Don't expect the student to be working solidly through the revision and examination period because that would be an inefficient studying approach, as is explained in this book.
- Say clearly what you are prepared to offer in the way of help.
- The essence of helpful listening is that you are attentive and accept what the student says, without moralising or judging. Keeping their confidences to yourself, you enable them to express exactly how they feel, think and behave, without comparing them with others.

**TALK ABOUT YOUR PROBLEM**

Ask your helper to be an attentive listener for you. Negotiate the kind òf help you would like. Here are two suggestions for you to consider.

### Listen without speaking

Ask your partner to say nothing, simply give you their undivided attention. Ask them to encourage you to talk by non-verbal signals e.g. smiles, nods, eye contact, touch and to allow you to display any emotion you feel.

Talk for as little or as long as you like about any aspect of the problem that is uppermost in your mind. You could use parts of the book to give a focus to what you say, if you prefer. The exercise will give you an opportunity to listen to yourself.

At the end, you could summarise the main concerns you have expressed.

### Listen and summarise.

Use the above negotiated approach, asking your helper to be equally attentive and encouraging to you. This time, leave pauses in what you say and express, for your helper to summarise both the fact and the feeling in what you have said. If the helper doesn't summarise the essential meaning of what you have said, help by repeating what you expressed and giving your helper another chance to summarise it, in turn. Continue, using this approach, until you have been able to express all of the problem.

### Tackling the Problem

Use your helper to work through the four stages of the **Tackling the Problem** exercise by using either of the approaches from these two *Listening* exercises. The helper works with you, one stage at a time, to enable you to clarify what you can do about it and how you are going to do so. You could use the same approach to talk through the **Hierarchy of anxiety**.

### Using revision cards with a partner

Draw a diagram, make up a spider or patterned note card(s) or construct some linear key word notes.

Revise the card(s) for 15 to 20 minutes (at most). Re-check that you understand and can recall all of the card(s) contents.

Teach your partner about the topic, allowing — and encouraging — questions about the topic. When a point is unclear, stop and explain it. Work through the topic until you have both completed it to your satisfaction *or* have agreed to meet again to continue.

### Using your partner to fire questions

Work for a set period in your work room, e.g. ½ to 1 hour. Then ask your cooperative partner to fire questions at you about the topic. It will obviously help if the partner had some knowledge about the topic or a clear indication of what to ask. However, what you are seeking from this exercise is to keep flexible and alert to surprise questions and fresh angles are a bonus from this method.

### 'Test Me'

An additional option for the **Basic Revision Method** is to explain what you have been reading and learning to your partner. Alternatively, pass your partner your notes and ask to be tested on your understanding. 'Test me' is one of the commonest forms of using others as helpers and is as useful as it ever was.

## USING MORE THAN ONE HELPER FOR REVISION

### Conducting a seminar

One person in a group of 3, 4, 5 or 6, explains a topic to others. They can then ask questions, debate your points, give their own ideas, etc.

This technique has been very successful for a number of students I know and is highly recommended by them.

You can use this idea of marking and commenting on each other's work in a number of ways:—

— on presentations to a seminar.

— on introductions or conclusions to a topic, written or spoken.

— on the clarity and evidence of revision notes, particularly **Key word revision cards** (N.B. most cards are prepared for yourself. They may need amendment for presentation to others).

— on short, or outline answers to questions. A photocopy of each, marked silently, marks announced and then discussed, is particularly effective. (Examiners use the same techniques when they meet at Standardisation meetings to ensure they are marking in the same way, to the same standard and have grasped all the points for which marks may be awarded.)

### Brainstorming

Choose a topic or question which has a large number of aspects to it. Questions involving *solutions, consequences, results* or which ask you to offer *explanations* are particularly appropriate.

In your group, negotiate for one person to record information for the group. This may be on a tape recorder, in linear note form or patterned notes on a large sheet of paper or a piece of A4 paper. The recorder has the essential role of recording *every* point made by other group members.

Each member of the group, including the recorder, now has the opportunity to offer their solutions, explanations, etc. The ideas should come as quickly as possible. All of them must be recorded no matter how absurd or funny another group member may find them. No member of the group is allowed to criticise another member's ideas. The recorder should intervene if this happens and stop the rule breaker. Once all the ideas are recorded (the recorder can give interim summaries of what has been written down if this method is being used) the whole list can be opened up for debate and criticism and evaluation. In this way, all the ideas have been heard before any evaluation occurs and a wider perspective has been thrown on the question.

### The five-minute lecture

Prepare your topic by listing the major points you would wish to make in answer to a question. Talk about them, briefly, without elaboration, detail, detour or examples for exactly five minutes.

Invite your group to ask questions. Each member may ask only one question at a time, in turn. Your should make your answers brief — one word, one phrase, one sentence answers. The object is to maximise participation and to generate a large number of questions and thus stimulate every member's thinking about the topic.

# Bibliography

Bird, C. and Bird, D.M. — 'Learning More Effective Study'. New York. Appleton Centurn-Crofts, 1945, pp. 195-8.

Dryden, Windy — 'Examination Anxiety: What the Student Counsellor Can Do'. British Journal of Guidance and Counselling, Vol. 6, No. 2, July, 1978.

Gramonsway, G.N. and Simpson, J. — The Penguin English Dictionary, London Penguin Books, 1969.

Gibb, G. — Teaching Students to Learn. A student-centred approach. Milton Keynes Open University Press, 1981.

Goldman, Gloria — 'A contract for Academic Improvement' in Hills, P.J. (ed.), (1979), pp. 64-74.

Hamblin, D.H. — 'Teaching Study Skills'. Oxford. Blackwell, 1981.

Hills, P.J. — 'Study courses and counselling. Problems and possibilities'. Society for Research into Higher Education Monograph (1979).

Mace, C.A. — 'The Psychology of Study'. London. Penguin Books (Revised Ed.), 1962.

Marland, Michael — Information Skills in the secondary curriculum. London. Schools Council/Methuen Educational, 1981.

Michelbaum, D. — Self-Instruction methods (How to do it) in Goldstein, A. and Kaufer, F. (eds) 'Helping People Change: Methods and Materials', New York. Pergamon Press, 1975.

Roberts, M.M. — 'Establishing a Study Skills Course for Sixth-form Students'. Educational Research, volume 24, Number 1, November, 1981.

Rowntree, D. — 'Learn How to Study'. London. MacDonald and James (Revised Ed.), 1976.

Seymour, R. and Acres, D. — 'General and Liberal Studies: A Teacher's Handbook'. London. Darton Longman and Todd, 1974.

Tabberer, R. and Allman, J. — Study Skills at 16 Plus. Research in Progress, No. 4, NFER, 1981.

Tremlett, Dr. R. — 'Some Guidelines on Study Methods: Sitting Examinations'. Aston University. Prepared by Dr. Tremlett at the Polytechnic of the Southbank. Internally printed leaflet.

Wilby, Peter — 'How to win at exams: all the things you really need to know'. London. Sunday Times Colour Supplement, 16 May, 1982, pp.26-38.

Ansell, Gwen, 'Make the most of your memory' National Extension College 1984. Looks at all aspects of memory in a clear, practical way.

Ashman, S. and George A., 'Study and Learn' London. Heinemann 1982. The best book on studying available at present. Highly recommended.

Burgen, A.D. 'How to Study' A Practical Guide'. —London. Harrap 1982. A small, clear, useful and cheap guide to the process of study.

Burnett, Janis, 'Successful Study. A handbook for students'. London. Teach Yourself Books 1979. A useful, comprehensive book.

Buzan, Tony, 'Use Your Head'. London. BBC Publications 1974. Very good on creative patterns and certain kinds of memorising.

Cassie, W.F. and Constantine, T. 'Students Guide to Success'. London. MacMillan Press 1977. A useful and easy to read book, written by two Engineers.

Davies, Don 'Taking Examinations — Maximising Examination Performance'. A 33 minute audio-cassette tape designed to reduce stress and build confidence, costing £12.50 (inc. p. and p.) available from: Performance Programmes, 16 Priory Road, Malvern, Worcestershire, WR14 3DR. Telephone Malvern (06945) 5798.

De Larrabeiti, 'Full Marks, The Papermate Guide to Punctuation'. London. Mac-Millan Education 1981. A comprehensive guide to punctuation.

Eagle, R., 'Taking the Strain'. London. BBC Publications 1982. A very useful guide to a wide range of alternative stress coping techniques. Among them Autogenic training, yoga, meditation, biofeedback and massage. Clear explanations and a list of further courses, equipment and reading available.

Edwards, Betty, 'Drawing on the right side of the brain' Souvenir Press 1981. Looks at ways of using the creative, free-flowing mental faculties.

Freeman, R., 'Mastering Study Skills' Mac-Millan 1982. Includes some useful guidelines on thinking and arguing effectively.

Hittleman, R. 'Yoga for Health'. Hamlyn 1971. A very good basic yoga book.

Lorayne, H. and Lucas, J. 'The Memory Book'. London. Star Books W.H. Allen 1974. An American best-seller of memorising techniques.

Marshall, Lyn. 'Wake up to Yoga'. Ward Lock 1975. A very clearly illustrated yoga book. There are several records available by Lyn Marshall, one of which has the same title.

Millard, L. and Tabbener, R. 'Help yourself to Study' Longman 1985. A small, clear book giving practical exercises on such topics as finding information.

Open University, 'How to Study'. Milton Keynes, Open University Press 1978, and Open University 'Preparing to Study'. Milton Keynes, Open University Press 1979. Both these books are good quality guides for students returning to study, particularly with the Open University.

Rowntree, D., 'Learn how to Study'. London. MacDonald. (Revised Edn.) 1976. One of the best books published on studying techniques in recent years. A programmed text. Very good guidelines on taking examinations.

Temple, M., 'Get it right'. London. John Murray 1978. A very useful, clear and cheap guide to spelling grammar and punctuation rules.

The Association of Hypnosis and Psychotherapy, 25 Market Street, Nelson, Lancs. BB9 7LP. Telephone: 0282 699378. Hypnosis is a useful and effective aid for a wide range of stress. Approach the above Association to find members in your area and for further information.

Whale, John, 'Put it in writing' Dent 1984. An excellent book comprised of 34 small, clear, simple and effective chapters each on a specific aspect of writing.

Yendell, Penny, 'Taking the Strain'. Disc. No. REC 407. Cassette No. ZCM 407. BBC Records 1982. An LP and cassette of a relaxation course featured in the BBC series of the same name.

# Index